Robert Brown

Landscape Assessment for Planning and Design

Robert Brown

Landscape Assessment for Planning and Design

Seeing the Landscape Again for the First Time

VDM Verlag Dr. Müller

Imprint

Bibliographic information by the German National Library: The German National Library lists this publication at the German National Bibliography; detailed bibliographic information is available on the Internet at http://dnb.d-nb.de.

Cover image: www.purestockx.com

Publisher:
VDM Verlag Dr. Müller Aktiengesellschaft & Co. KG, Dudweiler Landstr. 125 a, 66123 Saarbrücken, Germany,
Phone +49 681 9100-698, Fax +49 681 9100-988,
Email: info@vdm-verlag.de

Produced in USA and UK by:
Lightning Source Inc., La Vergne, Tennessee, USA
Lightning Source UK Ltd., Milton Keynes, UK
BookSurge LLC, 5341 Dorchester Road, Suite 16, North Charleston, SC 29418, USA

ISBN: 978-3-639-03032-7

Acknowledgements

I am deeply indebted to the many individuals who participated in the development of this book. Jeffrey Brown, Robert Corry, Natasha Kenny, Robert LeBlanc, Lee-Anne Milburn, Susan Mulley, Ron Stoltz, Joyce Tang, and Tory Young provided brilliant ideas, insightful suggestions, and informative critiques.

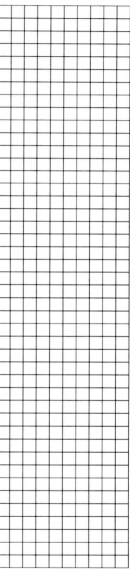

i

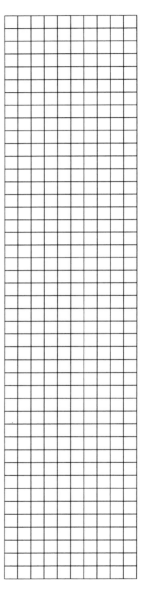

Table of Contents

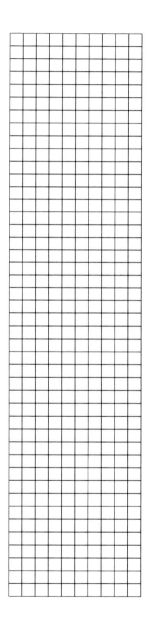

01 Introduction

Throughout your professional career you will be asked to make decisions about landscapes. It's very important that your recommendations are made with an understanding of the *structure* and the *function* of the many components of the landscape. While it's unrealistic to expect every landscape architect to have an in-depth understanding of every aspect of a landscape, it is realistic to expect that a landscape architect will be able to identify important components of a landscape and suggest how to appropriately use the land. Some aspects of the landscape are more important than others, and some elements are more affected by design modifications than are others. Some components are quite resilient and can withstand a lot of human use without adverse effects (*e.g.* a lawn), while other components are delicate and easily disturbed (*e.g.* moss).

This book will assist you as you learn about landscape - from theoretical foundations to practical applications. It provides an outline of what information is needed and what steps should be taken to help to ensure that important information is not missed, and that the important characteristics of the landscape are identified and illustrated in a form that will assist in planning and design.

Over the years I have spent many hours leaning over desks talking with individual students and small groups about recording and reporting field observations, constructing base maps, deciding what to do with maps of different scales, synthesizing landscape units and analyzing them in terms of capability and suitability, writing reports, and producing site reconnaissance reports. While I still intend to talk with individual students about all these things, this book should provide some of the background and step-by-step information that is often best learned by students working through it on their own.

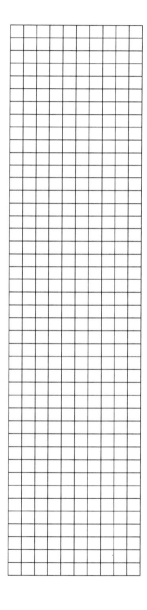

1

You will first be introduced to the concept of *process* as an integral aspect of site assessment. You will then be given an overview of each of the biological and physical resources of a landscape and how they all fit together to form a *system*. Then each resource will be discussed in more detail, with a focus on aspects that are most important when considering future land use. The next section will provide you with a series of *process guides* with step-by-step instructions on how to do things like collect data during a site visits or draw up a base map. The final section provides you with some approaches for using the site information when you are developing design recommendations.

By Thanksgiving you are going to sound soooo smart. As you are stuffing your face with turkey everyone around the table is going to know how much you have learned when you say something like "You really should have a longer overhang over your south-facing windows. It would allow solar radiation to provide passive heating in winter but block the direct solar radiation in summer. It would cut both your heating and cooling costs." And after dinner when you are walking off the pumpkin pie you might comment "That *Acer saccharum* looks like it is being crowded by the *Rhamnus cathartica* - I would suggest that you remove the *Rhamnus*."

So, c'mon. Let's get started.

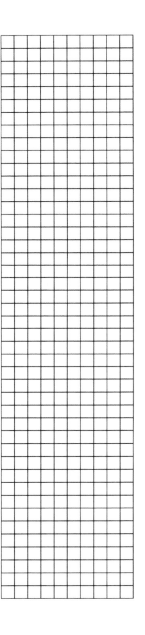

02 Process

The single most important aspect of landscape assessment is following a clear and defensible process. One way to think of process is that it is the series of steps that are taken. You could easily describe a process that you would follow to obtain a cup of coffee. One such process might involve the following steps:

1. *Enter a Tim Hortons;*
2. *Say to the clerk "large double double to go";*
3. *Read the number on the cash register and pay that amount to the clerk;*
4. *Receive your cup of coffee.*

You could follow this process several times, with very similar results every time. Other people could follow the steps that you have outlined and similarly be successful in obtaining a cup of coffee that is very similar to yours.

There are other processes that would also allow you to obtain a cup of coffee. For example, you could:

1. *Put some water into a kettle;*
2. *Plug in the kettle until the water inside is hot;*
3. *Put some instant coffee into a cup;*
4. *Pour some boiling water into the cup;*
5. *Add some cream and sugar and stir with a spoon.*

This process would also yield a cup of coffee. However, the product might not taste the same as that obtained through the first process, and might vary from time to time.

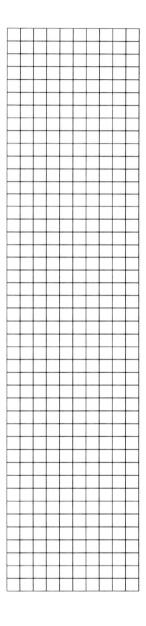

The Tim Hortons process could be said to be *reliable* because if you used this process over and over again, the results would be very similar. It could also be said to be *valid* as the process would yield a cup of coffee every time. These two measures, reliability and validity, give us confidence in the resulting product. The steps in the process are *clear and precise*, so someone else could reproduce our process with similar results. Finally, if you were to investigate the theory behind the way that Tim Hortons makes coffee you would find that they have studied the ideal water temperature for brewing coffee (water boils at different temperatures at different elevations, and water that is too hot will not make good coffee), the maximum length of time that coffee can be kept hot before it is no longer fresh (coffee is made up of a complex array of substances, some of which go rancid when kept warm for more than a short time), and so on. They have a strong theoretical basis for the decisions they have made, and thus the process they follow is *defensible*. That is, if someone challenged their approach to coffee-making they could defend themselves through the use of scientific theory and empirical results.

In contrast, the instant coffee process might provide something recognizable as coffee (thus would be somewhat valid) but there could be a wide range of results depending on how much water and coffee were added, the temperature of the water, and so on, thus the process would not be considered reliable. The steps are not clear and precise. For example, it is not specified how much water, or how much coffee. And finally, the process is not very defensible. The process that you follow is dependent on what is known as *empirical* evidence. You found through trial and error what the best combination is for you to make a cup of coffee. Empirical results are less defensible than theoretical and scientific results. If you were challenged in court, someone could follow the instant coffee instructions and come up with something barely resembling coffee. They could add a tiny amount of instant coffee crystals, a large amount of water, a lot of sugar and a tiny amount of cream. They could demonstrate that there were situations where your process didn't work, thus invalidating your argument.

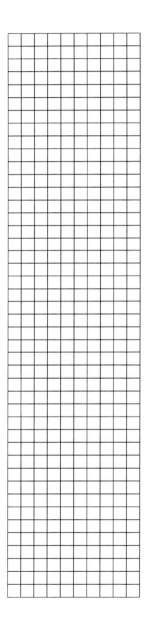

Now, if you haven't run out for a cup of coffee, let's try to see what this has to do with the landscape. Imagine that someone hired you to do an evaluation of a piece of land that they owned. If you followed a process that was similar to the instant coffee process, you might:

1. *Go have a look at the site and walk through it;*
2. *Draw some diagrams and write down what you see on the site;*
3. *Come up with some ideas how it could be used;*
4. *Develop a design for the site.*

This process might work for you once in a while, but there are many situations where you could run into trouble. For example, the client might attempt to go ahead with the plan only to have a local conservation group challenge the design on the grounds that it is an important breeding ground for the Five-Lined Skink (*Eumeces fasciatus*). If you ended up being sued in court, and the judge asked you to describe the process that you followed to ensure that your design avoided impacting the Five-Lined Skink, you would be unable to defend yourself. Similarly, if the client felt that you hadn't identified the true potential of the site, and hired someone else to use your process to check your results, they would likely come up with something very different. There is so much room for subjectivity throughout the process that the results would vary from time to time and from person to person.

If you did the same project, but used the Tim Hortons approach instead, the process might be:

1. *Accumulate and study all maps, air photos, and publications that are relevant to the site;*
2. *Visit the site and use field study to check that the published data are accurate and precise as well as learn anything else you can about the site through observation, measurement, and talking with local residents;*
3. *Consult with appropriate experts on any aspect of the site that appears to be sensitive or important and that is beyond your own expertise;*
4. *Write a clear and concise report that identifies for the client all the important aspects of their site, as well as the opportunities and constraints that this information yields, plus a proposal for how the site could be developed.*

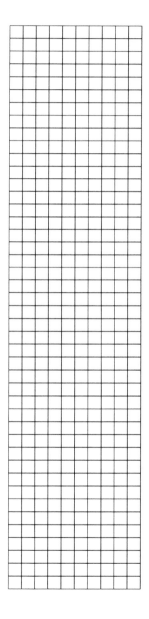

5

Chances are that through this process you would identify early on that there was a breeding ground for Five-Lined Skinks, and consider this as both an opportunity (for conservation and education) and a constraint (no modifications should be proposed for that part of the site), and probably avoid a lawsuit. The client would likely be very satisfied with your product, but if they did hire someone else to repeat your study, the result would likely be very similar to what you provided in the first place.

Probably in the back of your mind you have this little voice saying "Hey, I thought landscape architecture was a creative profession - where's the creativity in all this?" Some people might think that if you follow too strict a process that it will limit the opportunities to provide creative input. This is not the case. There are times for creative input, and times for solid scientific grounding. For example, there is no sense coming up with a very creative way to use the site for geodesic housing when you are going to either destroy Five-Lined Skink breeding habitat by doing it, or be stopped trying. Following a clear, reliable, valid, and defensible process will allow you to set the bounds within which you can be creative. As most creative people have found out, it can be most difficult to be creative if given too much freedom. It can be very difficult to come up with a creative idea when given a blank piece of paper. However, providing guidelines or limitations to a problem often leads to the most creative responses. Don't think of the landscape analysis process as limiting your creativity. Think instead of it providing the framework through which you can be sure that your creativity will not be wasted.

Notes:

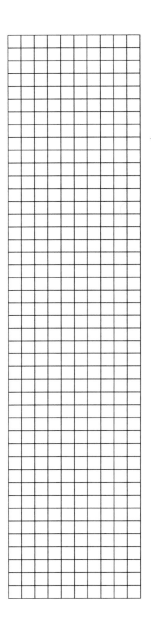

Process for Landscape Assessment

Every landscape is unique, so the steps for assessing each one of them cannot be identical as they were in the Tim Hortons coffee example. However, steps can be quite clearly set out so that, although the product will be different, the important aspects of each landscape will be identified and considered.

The first step of the process requires an investigation of information that has been published about a site. You should be able to find maps and reports or publications that illustrate and explain the landforms, surface water, vegetation, animals, soil, climate, and current land use of your site. These will be available in the local library, the internet, or through government offices. Normally these will be produced at a scale that provides a general view of these characteristics over a fairly large area, so the detailed information specific to your site will likely not be gained in this way. These maps will however provide you with the context of your site, a very important consideration.

The second step in the process is to acquire air photographs of the site and the area around the site. You should find *stereo pairs* - photographs taken from an airplane that allow you to look at your site as if it were in three-dimensions. This is a quick and easy way to become familiar with your site before leaving the office. It gives you a view as though you were floating over your site. You will readily be able to identify roads, structures, forested areas, and rivers. As you get more familiar with the process you will also be able to identify species of trees, and heights of buildings. There is a lot of information that can be gained through the use of air photos.

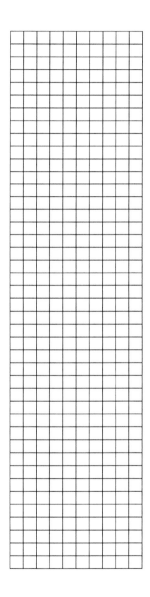

The third step involves taking copies of the maps and air photos and spending some time on the site. You should first walk around the site and visit the various features that you were able to identify on the air photo. This will allow you to 'ground truth' the information to make sure that nothing has changed since the photos were taken and the maps were produced. It also allows you to update the detail of the information. For example, there might be a small wetland on your site that doesn't appear on any maps or the air photo, but you are able to identify on the site. At this time you can collect information on any or all components of the site (*e.g.* conduct a species-composition study of the vegetation, talk to local residents about their preferences, *etc.*).

Step four requires that you begin to develop maps of the different elements of the site. You should consider producing a map for each of: landforms, soils, hydrology, vegetation, wildlife, microclimate, and land use, as well as anything unique or important about the site. Some of these maps can be combined in some circumstances – such as when the elements are closely connected or closely affect each other. For example you might decide that landforms and soils can be on the same map. Similarly hydrology and microclimate might share a map, as might vegetation and wildlife. Land use might become more than one map, again depending on the circumstances of the site. If there has been little previous use of the land, this information might be included in the landforms and soils map. If there has been much relevant use of the land by humans you might have an archaeological map, a historical land use map, and a current land use map.

Along with each map, step five involves writing a short and concise summary of the process that was followed to acquire the information in the maps, as well as a description of the various resources as a supplement to the map. This should include any information that might be relevant to future decisions about the site. The completion of this step essentially completes the *inventory* part of the landscape assessment process. The next steps involve the *analysis* part of the process.

Once the maps and descriptions have been prepared, the next step involves the synthesis of the information. This can be done through a variety of methods, but we will use a process that is very defensible: the identification and evaluation of *landscape units*. These are areas on the site that are relatively homogeneous from one side to the other. For example, there will be areas where the vegetation, wildlife, soil, and landform are quite similar throughout. These landscape units are identified and mapped on single map.

The final step of the analysis involves setting up a matrix and determining the capability and suitability of each of the landscape units. The capability is the inherent capacity of an area to be used for different activities, determined in as unbiased and objective a manner as possible. For example, a mature forest has the capability, from an objective point of view, to be used for industrial development. The mature forest could quite easily be removed and the site readily prepared for development. The suitability of the site considers the more value-laden and subjective aspects of the site. The mature forest might have considerable value as an ecosystems and you might want to make the argument that it would be more appropriate to preserve or conserve this use. By separating the capability and suitability, you can focus on the key aspect of your recommendation. You won't be put in a position to argue that the land *could* not be used for industrial development, only that it *should* not be used for that purpose.

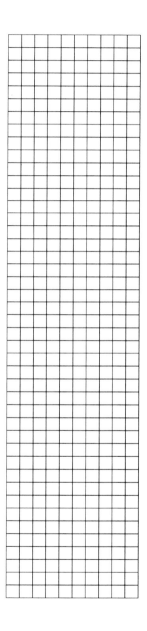

9

The results of the capability and suitability analysis should be drawn up as a map, showing your recommendations for the most appropriate uses of the various parts of the site. This map and the accompanying report become an integral part of the subsequent design process. If the client has identified a program of use, this is the time to begin to resolve the various uses desired by the client with the potential of the land to support those uses. From this point on, the creative processes take precedent throughout the planning and design process, but with the backing of a solid, scientifically based landscape assessment. It is very important that the landscape assessment is not simply set aside, having been completed. You completed it for a very important reason - to provide a solid basis for design decisions that are appropriate to the landscape, and as a measure of whether suggestions by the client, the public, or elected officials are appropriate. Use the landscape assessment maps and report as an integral component throughout the rest of the design of the site.

So those are the basic steps that you should follow in every planning or design project that you do. Now that you have that in hand we'll have a look at the landscape itself.

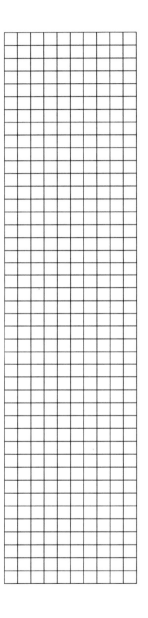

03 Components of the Landscape

An important concept to keep in mind at all times is that the landscape is not static. It has evolved over time and is still evolving – quickly in some ways and much more slowly in others. Toward the slower end of the scale is soil formation which can be as slow as one centimetre per thousand years. A process toward the faster end of the scale might be a flooded river cutting off a meander to form an *oxbow* lake in a matter of minutes. One of the challenges of landscape planning and design is to ensure that proposed land uses fit into these natural evolutionary processes.

One of the most valuable skills you will learn is how to *read a landscape*. There are clues in every landscape that, if interpreted properly, can tell what kinds of materials the soil is made of, what kinds of ecosystems occur naturally, and so on. This information will provide a valuable basis for making land use decisions.

Sometimes the answer will be obvious but others will be more difficult to read. Suppose that you were asked to analyze three different landscapes as potential sites for a housing development. The first site might be a flat area covered with Cattails (*Typha latifolia*) and Willows (*Salix spp.*). You would probably recognize this as a wet area and you would understand that there would be severe limitations if trying to develop this land for housing. Now let's turn to the other two sites, which might be more difficult to read.

To the untrained eye the second site might simply appear to be a group of trees. However, as you learn to read the clues you might recognize that the trees are mostly Sugar Maples (*Acer saccharum*) and American Beech (*Fagus grandifolia*). This combination of trees typically occurs on deep, rich, well-drained soils – ideal for housing development.

You might then notice that there is a small number of trees per unit area, and that each tree is quite large. This would likely indicate that it is a fairly mature forest and is potentially a very valuable ecological resource and not just a bunch of tree.

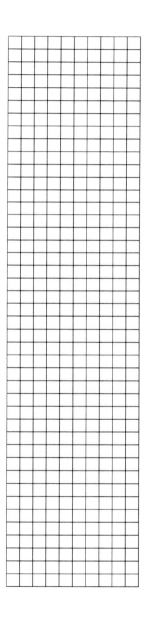

The third site is another forest but this time you can see that it consists primarily of Buckthorn (*Rhamnus cathartica*) around the outside and mostly Norway Maple (*Acer platanoides*) trees in the middle. Your knowledge of plants would allow you to see that these are both non-native, invasive species and have little ecological value. On first assessment, this is definitely the best site for the housing development.

One effective way to learn these valuable *landscape-reading* skills is to separate the landscape into components or layers and study each component of the landscape in turn. Each component has key indicators that say a lot about the landscape. Just like a Maple-Beech forest can indicate deep, rich, well-drained soils, there are many other characteristics that allow a landscape to be read.

Looking at a landscape with an untrained eye can be like trying to read Japanese for the first time. When you first see written Japanese it can be very difficult to understand it in any way. But by separating it into easy-to-learn components, like components of the landscape, it's actually not too difficult.

First you need to learn that written Japanese sentences don't go horizontally across a page, but rather vertically and are read from top to bottom. That makes the page a little more legible – at least you can see the order in which the symbols are to be read. It is then very valuable to learn that written Japanese consists of three alphabets, each with their own unique set of characters. Who knew!? At first they all look alike, but once each set is separated out it is actually quite easy to recognize which of the alphabets is being used.

Investigating each of the alphabets in turn allows you to see that two of the three alphabets are actually quite easy to learn and to read. Each symbol stands for a sound, such as sue, or she. One of the alphabets, known as *katakana*, is used almost exclusively to write words that are not traditional Japanese words – words like whisky or California. Once you know this trick, whenever you see that alphabet used you can work out the word phonetically and it will sound very similar to the non-Japanese word. A very valuable thing to know!

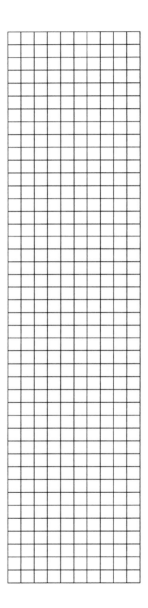

Another of the alphabets, *hiragana*, is also a phonetic alphabet so these letters can be used to read many common Japanese words. I learned early on that two characters, one that sounds like *sue*, and the other that sounds like *she*, when found together on a sign would identify a place where I could get my favourite lunch – sushi!

Even though it can take a very long time to become an expert at reading Japanese, this basic understanding can allow a westerner to live quite easily and comfortably in Japan. When more detail was needed, a Japanese native could be called on to provide further interpretation or depth of understanding.

This is very analogous to reading a landscape. You can quite easily learn a couple of the *alphabets* of nature that will allow you to see many of the big concepts and to find your way around. When you need more detail or more depth of understanding, there are experts that can be called upon to provide this – geomorphologists, pedologists, all kinds of scientists that can tell you what you need to know.

The next section is going to introduce you to the various *alphabets* of the landscape – the landforms, climate, water, plants, animals and soils. The first time through will be an overview of how they all fit together (like learning that Japanese runs vertically down the page and is made up of three alphabets), and the second time through will be a bit more detail of what you need to know about each of the resources - like knowing the symbols for su and shi and how to recognize them on signs.

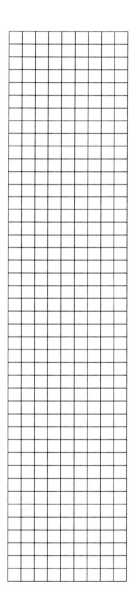

Landscape Evolution

The landscapes of most of Canada are quite young in comparison with many parts of the world. A continental glacier that covered almost all of Canada completely reworked the landscape as recently as 6,000 to 10,000 years ago (Figure 01). Pre-glacial landforms, vegetation and animals were displaced or destroyed, and when the glacier melted it left behind a completely new surface on the landscape. Climate interacted with the new landforms to create microclimates that allowed specific kinds of plants and animals to survive. The interactions between landforms, plants, and animals led to the development of different types of soils. Humans have been part of the Canadian landscape since the time of the glacier, but their impact has increased over time.

Notes:

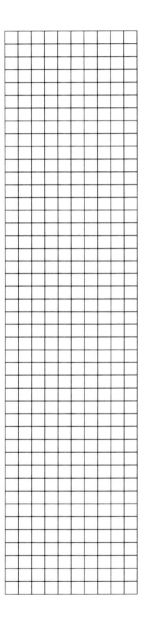

Figure 01 -

This series of drawings illustrates how: (a) the overall shape of most of the land in Southern Ontario was formed by glaciers about 6,000 years ago, (b) these landforms interacted with climatic elements of solar radiation and rain, creating some environments that were cooler and moister (slopes facing to the north), and some that were warmer and drier (slopes facing to the south), (c) different kinds of vegetation prefer different kinds of heat and moisture conditions, so different kinds of plants grew on the north-facing compared with the south-facing slopes, (d) similarly different species of animals inhabit the north-facing compared with the south facing slopes, (e) different kinds of soils formed on the different slopes and orientations, and (f) humans have had a substantial impact on virtually all aspects of the ecosystem.

Notes:

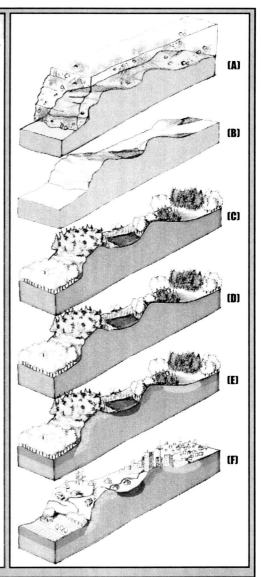

(A)

(B)

(C)

(D)

(E)

(F)

Almost all landscapes in Canada have, as their foundation, a geological or glacial process that deposited materials on the surface of the earth (Figure 01a). This resulted in identifiable forms on the landscape. It's a bit like when your dorm room gets particularly messy. After things like sneakers, crushed beer cans, and pyjamas are strewn all over the floor, some mornings the sheet that slid off in the middle of the night covers them all. Despite everything being completely covered by a sheet, you would still be able to recognize the sneakers (sloping hills, steep at one end), the beer cans (tall steep hills if standing up, low rounded hills if laying on their side), and the pyjamas (rumpled hills with no particular pattern). These are similar to forms that can be seen in the landscape. The messy glacier left low sloping hills steep at one end that we now call *drumlins* and once you learn to recognize them you will be able to easily identify them.

Notes:

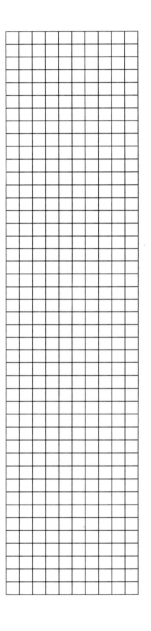

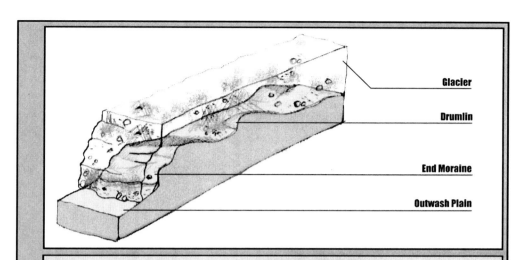

Glacier

Drumlin

End Moraine

Outwash Plain

Figure 01 a - Glaciation

Southern Ontario was covered by a glacier that formed most of the landforms we now see.

Notes:

Glacially-deposited landforms have been acted upon by climate and water, creating microenvironments that allow different species of plants to survive (Figure 01b). Continuing with the messy room example... imagine turning on your desk light in the corner of your room. The side of the sheet hills facing toward the light would be quite bright, and the sides facing away would be quite a bit darker. Now imagine that your hamsters have escaped their cage and are now *free-range hamsters*. If hamsters are late risers (having been running on their hamster wheel all night) they might want to continue sleeping in the morning when you turn on your desk light, and would definitely want to be on the shady side of the hills so the light doesn't shine in their eyes and wake them up. If you also had a free-range snake it might prefer to wake up early and to use the light from the lamp to heat itself up, so would sleep on the side of the hills that got more light in the morning.

Notes:

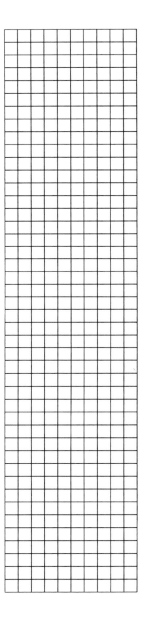

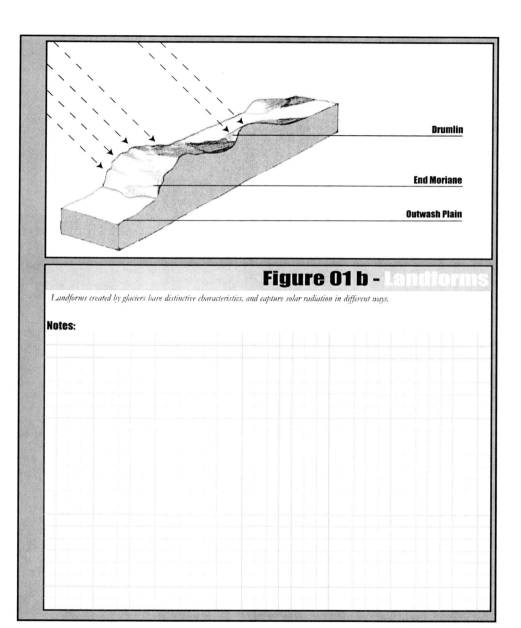

Drumlin

End Moriane

Outwash Plain

Figure 01 b - Landforms

Landforms created by glaciers have distinctive characteristics, and capture solar radiation in different ways.

Notes:

Plants will tend to grow in microenvironments that best meet their needs. Just like the hamsters liked the shady side of the hills, these cool and moist microenvironments provide locations for plants like Eastern Hemlock (*Tsuga canadensis*), and the bright side of the hill that the snake preferred provide a warmer and drier microenvironments that are preferred by plants like White Pine (*Pinus strobus*) (Figure 01c).

Notes:

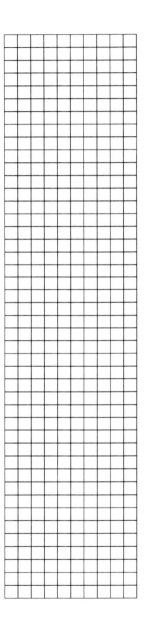

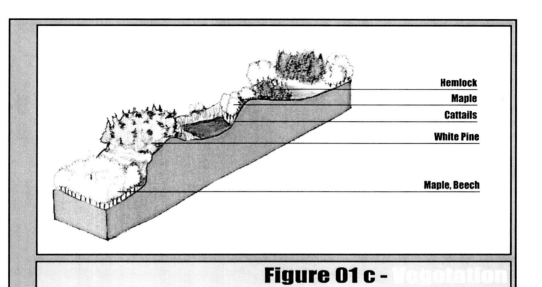

Hemlock
Maple
Cattails
White Pine

Maple, Beech

Figure 01 c - Vegetation

Plants will tend to grow in microenvironment that best meet their needs. White Pine trees are often found on dry south-facing slopes while Hemlock are often found on moist, north-facing slopes.

Notes:

In turn the plants affect their microenvironment and consequently influence the animals that can survive. Animals tend to live in environments that best meet their specific needs. Cool, moist Eastern Hemlock (*Tsuga canadensis*) woods might support the Eastern Garter Snake (*Thamnophis sirtalis sirtalis*), while warmer drier White Pine (*Pinus strobus*) woods might support the Eastern Massassauga Rattlesnake (*Sistrurus catenatus catenatus*). (Figure 01d).

Notes:

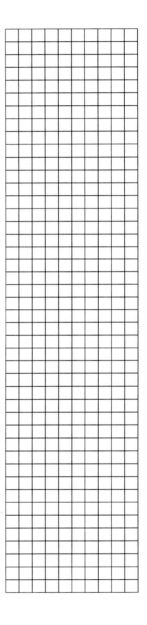

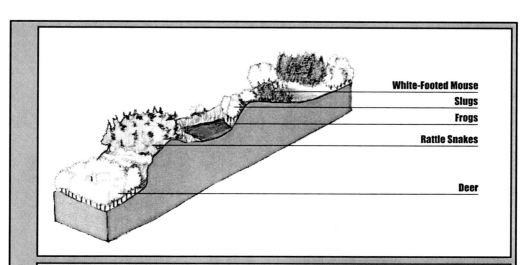

White-Footed Mouse
Slugs
Frogs
Rattle Snakes
Deer

Figure 01 d - Animals

Animals in the landscape tend to live in the ecosystem that best meets their specific needs. Some species require moist, shady environments while others prefer dry, sunny landscapes.

Notes:

Over time the interactions among the plants, animals, climate, water, and landform have created soils (Figure 01e). The result of these processes, over at least 6,000 years, is a series of dynamic ecological systems, or ecosystems, in which the structure and processes have interacted and remained dynamically stable over time.

Notes:

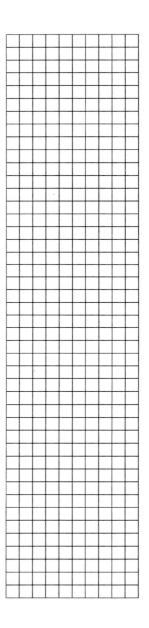

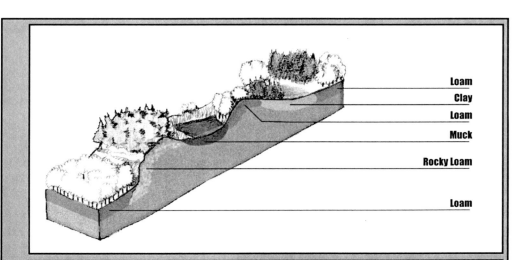

Loam
Clay
Loam
Muck
Rocky Loam
Loam

Figure 01 e - Soils

The type of soil found in each microenvironment is a function of the landform, microclimate, and vegetation over a long period of time.

Notes:

Humans then acted upon these six biological and physical (*bio-physical*) components of the landscape (landforms, climate, water, plants, animals, and soils) creating the social and cultural (*socio-cultural*) component of the landscape (Figure 01f). In most cases this human component began to interact with the other elements of the landscape shortly after the land was formed, but until about one or two thousand years before the present (B.P.) the impact of humans was not dissimilar to that of animals. However, in the past millennium or so, human impact has become greater than all other animals, and is now often considered as separate from nature.

The primary role of landscape architects is to make recommendations for appropriate use of land. These recommendations will be affected by economic, political, functional, social, cultural, aesthetic, and many other considerations. However, any recommendations for the use of land should, at its base, consider the biological and physical components, so that future uses of the land fit into the natural processes rather than working against them.

Now that you have the big picture overview of how the components of the landscape fit together, let's look at each of them in a bit more detail.

Notes:

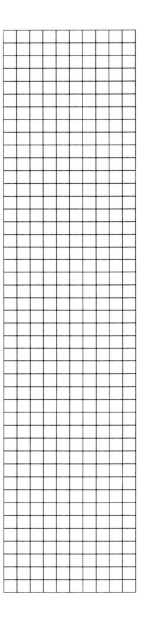

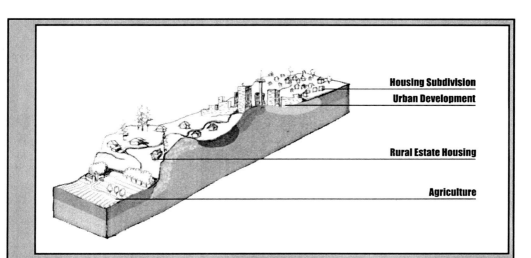

Housing Subdivision

Urban Development

Rural Estate Housing

Agriculture

Figure 01 f - Human Impact

Human use of the landscape is affected by the various characteristics. For example, it is much easier to build roads and cities on flat outwash plains than in rocky moraine.

Notes:

Landforms

No one alive today remembers what the lands of southern Canada looked like when they were first formed. Scientists have used good evidence to develop the theory that most of the landforms of southern Canada were created between six and ten thousand years ago. At that time a very large sheet of ice several kilometres thick, called a glacier, covered most of Canada. It is a bit difficult to conceptualize, but imagine a large bowl of firm jello being flipped over and set on a map of Canada (see Figure 02). If you pressed your hand on the middle of the resulting mound of jello some of the material would squoosh out the sides. This is much like the process that happened, in very slow motion, to much of southern Canada. As the jello squooshes over the map, it will pick up any dust or other materials on the map, and move them with it to the edges of the jello. When the glacier moved across the land, it picked up material from the surface of the land, carried it along, and deposited it at its edge.

Now imagine that as you are pressing down on the jello you put a heat lamp near the edge of the jello. The jello near the edge will melt and any material that it picked up, as it moved, will then either be set down on the map, or carried away by the melted jello as it runs off. This is very similar to the process that happened in southern Canada. The glacier melted at its edges and the material that it had picked up was deposited or was carried away by the melted glacier (called meltwater) and deposited elsewhere.

Notes:

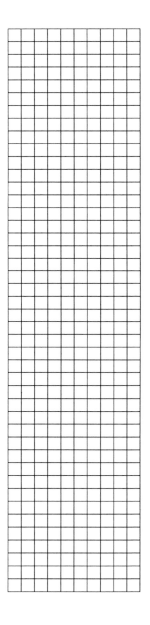

28

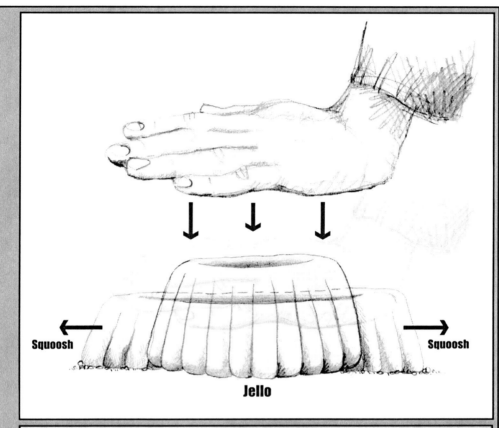

Squoosh

Jello

Squoosh

Figure 02 - Jello Analogy

The way that glaciers moved across the continent was similar to the way that a pile of jello would move if placed on a horizontal surface. The weight of the glacier forced it to flow out at the edges, similarly to the way that jello would flow out the sides if you placed your hand on top and pressed down gently.

Notes:

Water can carry materials as a function of its speed. The faster it is moving, the more and heavier the materials it can carry. As the glacial meltwater flowed over steep areas, it could pick up and carry almost any size of material, but as it reached flatter lands its speed would slow down. The first thing that fell out of the flowing water would be the heaviest material (see Figure 03). As the water slowed further, the next-heaviest materials would fall out, and so on. Many of the resultant landforms are composed of only one size of material, which is why we often find, for example, deposits of pure gravel in the landscape.

Notes:

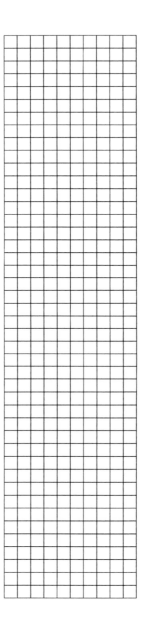

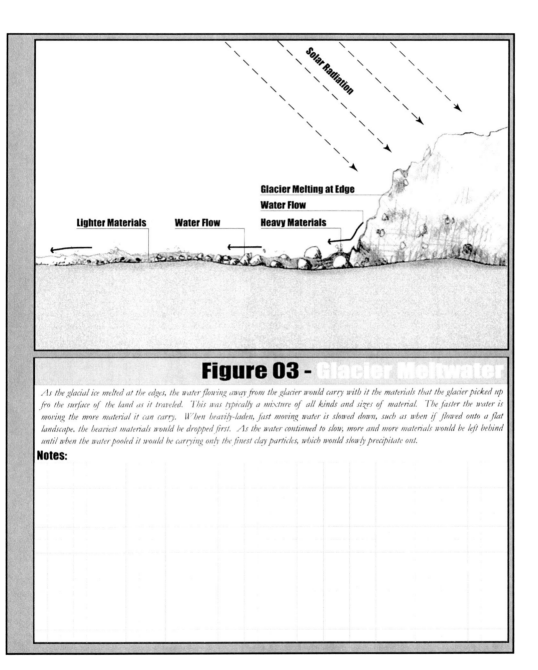

Figure 03 - Glacier Meltwater

As the glacial ice melted at the edges, the water flowing away from the glacier would carry with it the materials that the glacier picked up fro the surface of the land as it traveled. This was typically a mixture of all kinds and sizes of material. The faster the water is moving the more material it can carry. When heavily-laden, fast moving water is slowed down, such as when if flowed onto a flat landscape, the heaviest materials would be dropped first. As the water continued to slow, more and more materials would be left behind until when the water pooled it would be carrying only the finest clay particles, which would slowly precipitate out.

Notes:

The various landforms on a site are typically mapped by identifying the manner in which they were formed. For example, a glaciated landscape might have landforms called drumlins (formed by glaciers moving across the land), eskers (formed by water flowing under a glacier) and outwash plains (formed by water flowing out of a glacier) (see Figure 04). Each of these has typical characteristics that can be very useful in making planning and design decisions. For example, eskers will be primarily gravel, outwash plains will be sorted into areas of gravel and sand, and drumlins will usually be a jumble of everything mixed together.

Figure 04 illustrates four glacial landforms that are typically found in southern Canada. The first one is a drumlin (like your sneaker under the sheet) and is shaped like an upside down spoon. The University of Guelph is built on a field of drumlins. Johnston Hall is on top of a drumlin, and if you stand on the front steps you can see across to the next drumlin, the Dairy Bush Hill. The second illustrated landform is an esker. There are only a few of these left in the landscape because they consist almost entirely of sand and gravel, so have been removed for building materials. The third landform is a moraine which is like your pyjamas covered by the sheet. It is a bit of a rumpled landscape, and is made up of a mixture of materials. The final form in the figure is an outwash plain. There areas tend to be very flat and very well-drained so are excellent areas for human development. If you drive south from the University of Guelph on Gordon Street you will travel through a drumlin field, across an outwash plain, and then suddenly rise onto a terminal moraine.

One of the first steps in reading a landscape is to identify the landforms. Try to see past all the details of vegetation, buildings, roads, and see the basic form of the land. Does it look like a sneaker under a sheet? Maybe it's a drumlin. Does it look like your snake has gotten under the sheet – an esker. Pyjamas – terminal moraine. Bare floor – outwash plain.

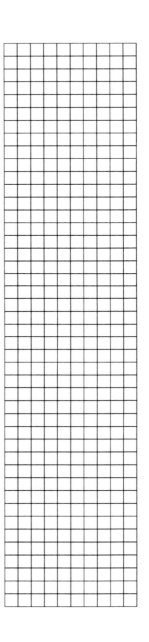

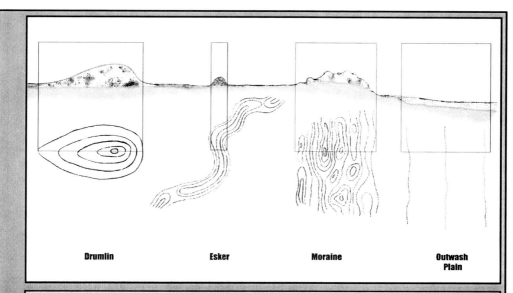

Drumlin **Esker** **Moraine** **Outwash Plain**

Figure 04 - Landform Structure

Here are four glacial landforms that we typically find in Southern Ontario. The first one is a drumlin and is shaped something like an upside down spoon (without the handle). The University of Guelph is built on a field of drumlins. If you stand in front of Johnston Hall and look across Gordon Street to the Dairy Bush Hill, you can see that it is a drumlin. You might also recognize that you and Johnston Hall are standing on another drumlin. The second from illustrated here is an esker. It is made almost entirely of sand and/or gravel, and for that reason most of the eskers in Southern Ontario have been completely removed to be used for construction materials. If you want to see part of an esker, there is part of one in Brown's Woods on campus. The third form is a moraine. This is the material deposited at the front edge of a glacier. It is a mixture of materials and tends to be 'rough' land. Drive south of campus on Gordon Street, and just as you reach Clair Road you drive up the face of a moraine. The fourth landform is an outwash plain. These areas tend to be good places for all kinds of human uses, including agriculture and settlement. If you drive south from Campus on Victoria Road and turn left on Arkell Road, you will be able to see a line of hills to your right (the moraine) and you will drive over a flat area that continues ahead and off to your left. This is an outwash plain, where the waters flowed off the moraines and spread out onto the landscape, depositing materials as it's velocity slowed.

Notes:

33

Climate

Intensity of solar radiation is the key mechanism by which climate affects a landscape. As the Earth revolves around the Sun, our perception in the northern hemisphere is that the sun is moving through the sky, rising in the eastern sky, passing its highest point in the south, and setting in the west (see Figure 05). In the southern hemisphere the sun still rises in the east and sets in the west, but travels through the northern sky.

Think back to your dorm room example, and imagine that you only have one light that you can turn on. In the morning you use the light on your desk at one end of your room, at noon you carry it over to the table in the middle of the room to have lunch, then in the afternoon you carry it over to the other end of the room so you can sit on the couch and do your readings for class. Your hamster, lying on the side of a sneaker facing away from your desk, would experience this as a cool and dark in the morning, lighter at mid-day, and brightest in the afternoon. The snake on the other hand, being on the other side of the hill, would have bright light in the morning (that it could use to heat up its body), moderate light at mid-day, and shady in the afternoon (so it wouldn't overheat). Different species of plants and animals have different needs for light at different times of the day, so would occupy different locations in the landscape. By knowing where the sun will be at any given time, and knowing the slope of the land and which direction the slope is facing, you can identify which species are likely to occupy different parts of the landscape. You can also use this knowledge to create habitat for animals in a landscape.

Notes:

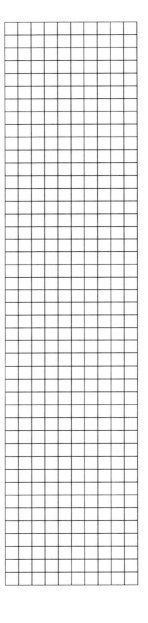

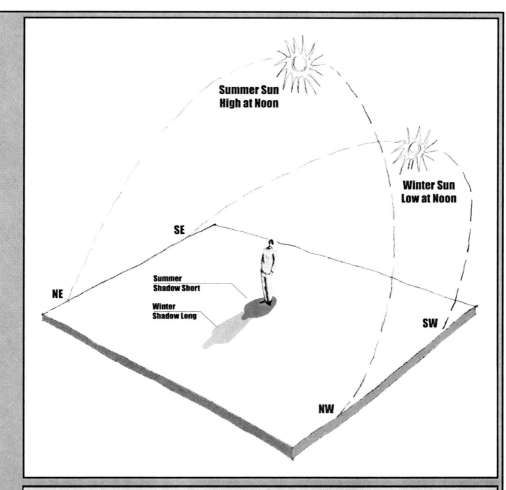

Figure 05 - Sun Angles

The sun moves in very predictable paths through the sky. In winter the sun rises in the southeast, and sets in the southwest without ever rising very high above the horizon. In summer, the sun rises in the northeast and sets in the northwest, and during midday is very high in the southern sky.

Notes:

Up to this point in your life you might have thought that what comes from the sun is just *light* but in fact only about half of the energy from the sun is in the form of light that our eyes can see. From now on you need to think of the energy from the sun as being *solar radiation* and you need to think of it as being half visible, and half invisible.

When solar radiation strikes a surface that is perpendicular to it, the intensity of the radiation received is at its highest. This is the point in the landscape that will have the highest input of energy from the sun, and this energy will be used to do things like evaporate water, heat up soil and so on. These points in the landscape tend to be warmer and drier than other areas.

If we take the opposite example where a surface is almost parallel to the direction of the solar radiation, the amount of energy per unit area can be very small. This means there is very little energy available to evaporate water or heat the surface, so these areas tend to be cooler and moister (see Figure 06).

This relationship has all kinds of implications for the landscape. First of all it is basically the driving force behind everything that happens in the landscape. If you have a tree that loves cool shady environments and you plant it on the hot, sunny, dry, south-facing side of a hill, it will have a hard time surviving. Then take the example of a person in the landscape. Imagine a hot sunny summer day. If you stood on the south side of a hill facing the sun you would be flooded with solar radiation which over time would make you feel very warm, probably even hot. However if you walked over the hill onto the north-facing side the amount of solar radiation both you and the surface would receive would be much less, and you would feel much more thermally comfortable.

The really cool thing is that as a designer you have control over where you put things in the landscape. If you remember this relationship between landform and sun you can put outdoor sitting areas in places that will be thermally comfortable for people. And you can plant trees and shrubs in locations that will be suited to their needs.

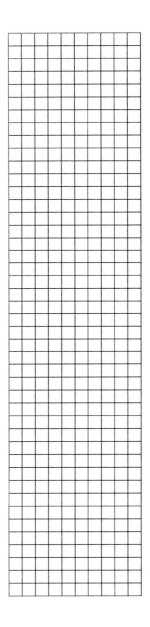

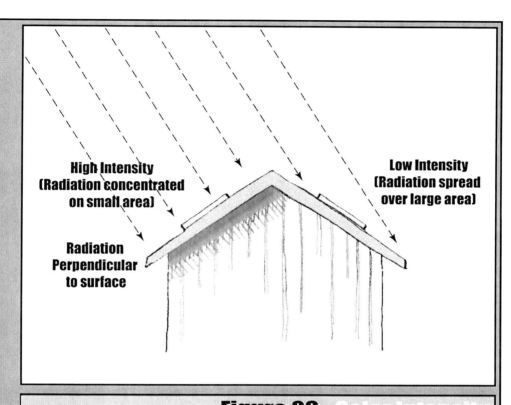

**High Intensity
(Radiation concentrated
on small area)**

**Low Intensity
(Radiation spread
over large area)**

**Radiation
Perpendicular
to surface**

Figure 06 - Solar Intensity

The more nearly the rays of the sun are to perpendicular to a surface, the higher the intensity of the radiation.

Notes:

We can say much of this in a bit more scientific way. That is, ground surfaces that slope towards the south will receive the highest intensity of solar radiation. When absorbed by the ground this radiation becomes either sensible heat (heat that we can sense) or latent heat (heat that is used to evaporate water). If there is no water available, then the entire amount of heat goes into heating the ground surface. This means that south-facing slopes will generally be warmer and drier than the average in the landscape (see Figure 07). Conversely, north-facing slopes will receive the lowest intensity of radiation, have the lowest amount of heat available, and will consequently be cooler and moister than the average.

When discussing the effects of climate on small areas such as this, we often use the term *microclimate*. It is very difficult to draw a map of the microclimate of a site as it is continually changing. As the sun moves through the sky different slopes have different relationships to the sun and the amount of heating is continuously changing. We resolve this difficulty by mapping, instead, the elements of the landscape that affect and modify the microclimate. A microclimate map often illustrates how steep a slope is, and also what direction the slope is facing – its *orientation* or *aspect*.

The effect of microclimate on vegetation can be quite dramatic. If you drive through the Qu'Appelle Valley in Saskatchewan during the summer you would see a distinct pattern. The slopes of the valley that are oriented toward the south and thus receiving high intensity solar radiation, are covered in grasses and these are often dry and brown by mid-summer. The slopes oriented toward the north, and thus receiving low-intensity solar radiation, are covered in trees and shrubs and are green all summer. The lower intensity of radiation allows the north-facing slopes to be cooler and moister, and consequently allowing trees and shrubs to grow.

Notes:

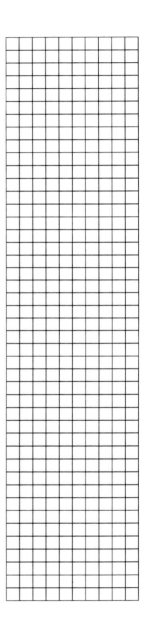

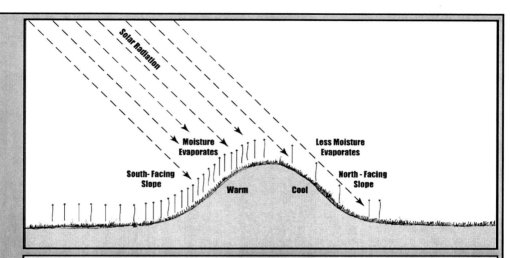

Figure 07 - Effect of Slope

Slopes facing to the south will be more nearly perpendicular to the rays of the sun, so will receive a higher intensity of radiation and will be hotter, thus causing more moisture to evaporate, and consequently are drier than flat areas. Similarly, north-facing slopes will be far from perpendicular to the rays of the sun, so will receive less intensity of radiation and will be cooler and moister than flat areas. The slope and orientation of the land has a substantial impact on all other aspects of the landscape.

Notes:

Water

You are probably familiar with the concept of the *hydrologic cycle* (see Figure 08). This is a very useful concept when assessing a landscape. Water moves through the landscape in very predictable ways. Precipitation will either be intercepted by elements in the landscape, infiltrate into the ground, or travel overland on the surface of the landscape.

While we know the general route that water takes, it is much more difficult to determine how long each of the legs of the journey will take, but most of the water that you will deal with will pass through your site in a matter of minutes to days or weeks. Some water that falls will be intercepted by leaves and might evaporate quickly back into the atmosphere. Other water that falls on the landscape will make the complete journey to the sea and might not make its way into the atmosphere again for a very long time.

Where the water flows to, and how it is used in the landscape, are major determinants of which plants and animals will live in different parts of the landscape. The type of soil and the slope of the land will both affect the amount of water that enters the soil and the amount that runs off. Soils with a large proportion of clay will become saturated quickly and most water will run off. Similarly compacted soils will not allow much infiltration, nor will impervious surfaces such as most asphalt and concrete. Low-lying areas, particularly those that have no outlet for the water to escape, will tend to be moist or even wet. There is a strong relationship between soils and water in the landscape. Soils of *light texture* will allow water to move through quite readily, while soils with *heavy texture* will not.

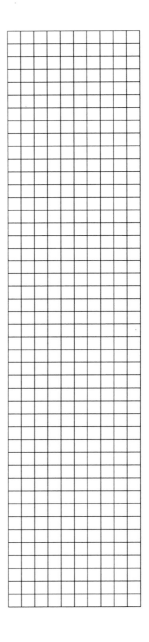

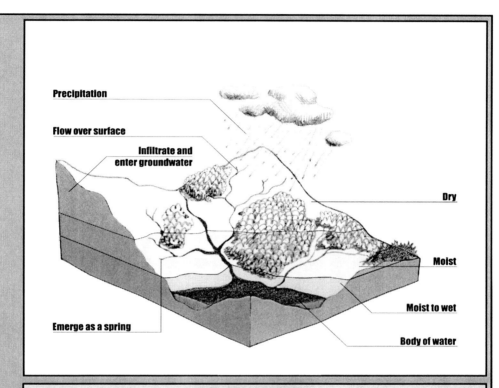

Precipitation

Flow over surface

Infiltrate and
enter groundwater

Dry

Moist

Moist to wet

Emerge as a spring

Body of water

Figure 08 - Hydrologic Cycle

You probably studied the 'hydrologic cycle' at some point in your schooling. Now you will be able to put this concept to good use. All water that reaches the surface via precipitation has to go somewhere. Some of it will evaporate back into the air, some will enter the ground, and some will run off. The water that runs off is normally of most interest to us. As it flows over the surface it can erode soil, carry pollutants (such as oil that has dripped from cars, or herbicides that have run off lawns, etc.) and deposit them in rivers, lakes, and groundwater. Where the moisture flows to, and how it is used by the environment, is a major determinant of which vegetation and animals will live in various places.

Notes:

Surface water that does not pond will continue to flow until it reaches a stream or river, and then will continue to flow in the waterway until it reaches a lake or the sea. These waterways cut through the landscape following the path of least resistance, and create identifiable landforms as they erode and deposit materials (see figure 09). Water moving over the surface of the land meanders back and forth, creating the familiar *winding river* form. The water on the outside of each meander moves faster than that on the inside of the curve. This faster moving water erodes the bank of the river, making the meander wider and wider. At the same time the slower moving water on the inside of the curve drops material and creates a deposition. In this way a river will meander back and forth, over time, across a landscape. There is no sense trying to stop this meandering – many people have tried many times, with some spectacular failures. Rather you should incorporate this mechanism into landscape designs.

When you map hydrology, you should typically illustrate the steepness of slopes, the areas where congregated water flows overland in streams and rivers, areas of surface water such as lakes and wetlands, and, if the information is available, you should also illustrate the depth to groundwater and the directions of flow of the groundwater.

There are several water-related things you can look for when reading a landscape. Vegetation is often a very good environmental indicator. Plants will grow only where the conditions are appropriate, and many species of plants have specific moisture requirements. Natural drainage channels are also worth noting. You will see these as small valleys in a hillside where water flows during storms or snowmelt events. It is critical to keep these channels free of obstructions – so they are definitely not a good place to put a building! Also look for areas that are greener or browner than surrounding areas. Sometimes you can see these on site, and sometimes on air photos or satellite images. Greener areas will sometimes indicate an abundance of water while browner areas often indicate a water restriction of some kind. This can be critical information when considering what vegetation to plant in an area.

Notes:

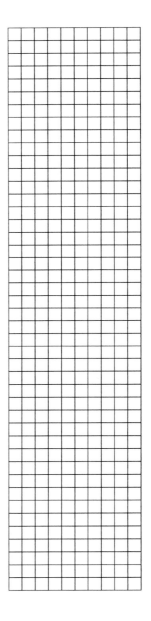

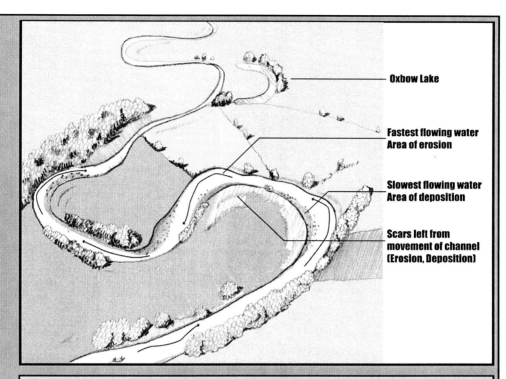

Oxbow Lake

Fastest flowing water Area of erosion

Slowest flowing water Area of deposition

Scars left from movement of channel (Erosion, Deposition)

Figure 09 - Characteristics of a River

As water moves over the surface of the land it tens to create identifiable patterns. For example, water flowing in channels such as rivers will tend to meander, flowing back and forth across the land. The water will erode material from the outside of curves in the river because this is where the velocity of the water is the highest. It will deposit that material on the insides of curves due to the slow velocity of the water at these points. In this way the river channel moves through the landscape.

Notes:

Plants

Material left by glaciers, microclimatic conditions, and moisture conditions will strongly influence what species of plants can grow in different microenvironments in a landscape (see Figure 10). Specific groups of plants tend to grow together in the landscape, and are often used to provide names for ecosystems. Some of the more familiar names that you might have heard of are the Maple-Beech forest (*Acer saccharum – Fagus grandifolia*) and the Cedar swamp (*Thuja occidentalis*).

When reading the vegetation of a site, start by looking for species that you recognize. With a little practice you will be able to recognize many of the typical tree species, such as Sugar Maples, American Beech, and so on. When first learning to identify plants, take a plant identification *key* along with you to the field. It will give you step-by-step instructions that will lead you to the plant name.

If you recognize a grouping of trees that you know typically grow together this will give you a template for other things you can look for. For example, if it is a Maple-Beech forest you would also expect there to be plants like Trillium (*Trillium grandiflora*) so could look for it. If it isn't there you can ask yourself why not. Alternatively you can look for plants that wouldn't naturally occur in this type of forest – such as Buckthorn or Norway Maple. If you find these you will know that the natural vegetation has been invaded by non-native species.

When developing maps of the vegetation of the site, start by identifying and outlining the main patterns. Separate the vegetation into categories based on their *structure*. Some typical structure categories are forest, woodlot, meadow, and cultivated lands. Each of these categories would warrant a separate colour on your map. Within each category you might have subcategories. For example, the forested area might have some forest that consists of deciduous trees and others that are mostly coniferous. And within a deciduous zone you might have some that is dominated by Sugar Maples and other areas dominated by White Ash (*Fraxinus americana*) trees. Some other typical characteristics used to map vegetation on a site include species composition, age, and species distribution.

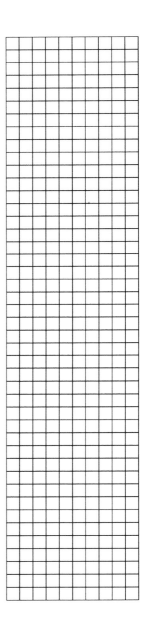

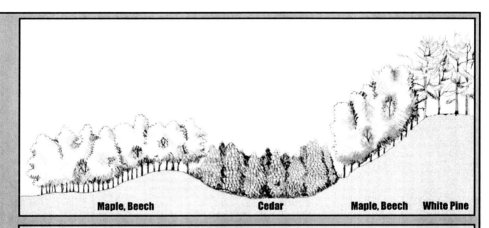

Maple, Beech   **Cedar**   **Maple, Beech**   **White Pine**

Figure 10 - Soils and Vegetation

Different species of vegetation tend to grow in specific environments. When a cross-section of a landscape is drawn, we often find a close relationship between the environmental conditions and the vegetation associations. For example, in low and wet areas we might expect to find Eastern White Cedar (Thuja occidentalis) trees, while on dry ridges we would be more likely to find Eastern White Pine (Pinus strobus), and on well-drained, rich soils in the middle we would expect to find Sugar Maples (Acer saccharum) and American Beech (Fagus grandifolia) trees.

Notes:

Animals

There is a very close relationship between the flora and the fauna in a landscape. Animals have specific needs for survival and reproduction, and different ecosystems tend to provide better habitat for some species than for others. There is much overlap, of course, but you tend to find certain species of birds in the interior of a forest, and others at the edge. Animals such as salamanders and frogs that need to be in a moist environment will not survive in the hotter, drier areas of a landscape.

Some animals also adapt better to human presence than others. For example, the American Robin (*Turdus migratorius*) is well adapted to human environments, while the Pileated Woodpecker (*Dryocopus pileatus*) needs interior forest habitat and is not successful near too many humans (Figure 11). Some animals are also more compatible with humans than are others. For example, people tend to be quite happy to see chickadees and butterflies, but do not want skunks or rats living nearby.

When reading the landscape there are many clues that indicate the presence of animals. You can look for twigs of trees that have been bitten off that can indicate a population of White-Tailed Deer (*Odocoileus virginiana*). You can listen for bird calls, or look for animal droppings, tracks in soft or wet soil, or areas where a burrowing animal has thrown soil onto the surface. And don't forget insects. Look for cocoons or ant hills, or butterflies. Many animals are very difficult to detect so you will often have to rely on the vegetation patterns to indicate whether you might expect different species of animals. So when mapping the fauna of a site you can often combine it with the vegetation map, indicating either on the map or in the report they typical species of animals that would be expected in each vegetation category.

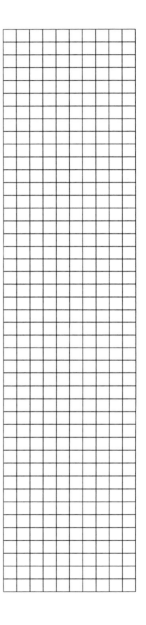

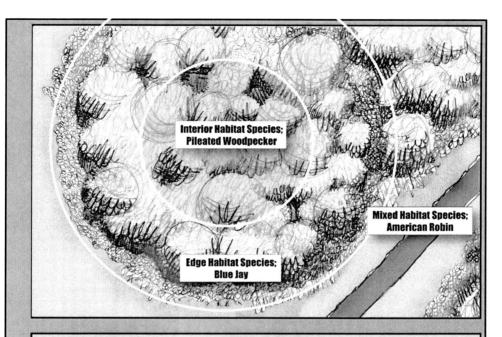

Figure 11 - Animal Habitat

Different species of animals tend to require specific environments. Some bird species, such as the Pileated Woodpecker, require habitat deep within a forest, while others such as the Blue Jay prefer habitat inside the forest but nearer the edge. Others, like the American Robin, prefer the outside edge of the forest and the surrounding open spaces.

Notes:

Soils

Soil is the result of many years of interaction among the landform, climate, water, vegetation, and animals in a landscape. Over time the various processes sort the material in the ground, add organic matter and nutrients, and eventually form a soil with a recognizable structure. You have already seen that low areas tend to have more fine particles, while hilltops tend to have less. Similarly, areas that support lush and dense vegetation tend to have more organic matter from the decaying leaves and plant materials.

One universal measure of soil is its *texture*. If you take a handful of soil and separate it out using a series of progressively smaller soil texturing screens, you will end up with three sizes of material: sand, silt, and clay (see Figure 12). The percentage of the soil that is composed of these various sized particles provides the name and identifiable characteristics of a soil. For example, a sandy soil will have mostly sand with little silt or clay. A loam soil has a mixture of the three sized particles.

The texture of the soil strongly influences its *drainage* ability – that is, how easily water can pass through it. A sandy soil doesn't hold water well and allows it to pass through quite readily. This can be an advantage if you want to be able to use an area shortly after a rain (*e.g.* golf greens, soccer fields) but can be a disadvantage in non-irrigated areas as it can be droughty in dry weather. Alternatively, clayey soils will hold water very well and in fact the clay particles absorb water and expand making the spaces between clay particles very small so little water can pass.

Notes:

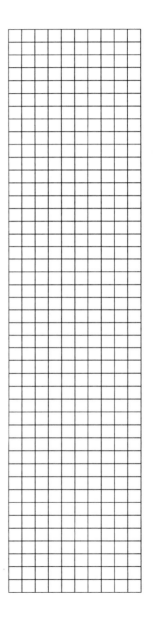

Sand

Silt

Clay

Figure 12 - Soil Characteristics

When soil is passed through a series of screens, starting with the one with the largest openings, it can be separated into its component particles: sand, silt, and clay. The percentage of the soil that is made up of these components determines what kind of soil it is. For example, a soil that is mostly sand will be called 'sandy', while one with an even mixture of the three particle sizes would be called 'loam'. Each type of soil has characteristics that make it more appropriate for different uses. Sandy soil doesn't hold water well, so would typically be droughty. However, it is a good medium for growing sod as long as it receives regular watering. Clay soils will expand when wet and contract when dry, so are limiting in terms of building on top of them. Clay soils also don't drain very well so are not appropriate locations for septic fields.

If you dig down through a soil, a clear and recognizable pattern of layers emerges (see Figure 13). The surface layer is known as the topsoil. This layer is where most of the organic matter accumulates, and where a vast array of micro-organisms lives. It is also the layer that provides many of the nutrients required by plants. Scientists call this the A-horizon. Below this is the second layer, known as the B-horizon, and below that is the C-horizon also known as the parent material. The material in the C-horizon has not been altered much since the glaciers laid it down.

With a little practice, reading the soils of a landscape can be quite easy. Scoop a bit of soil from the B-horizon, a piece about the size of a timbit, and roll it into a ball in your hand. Then toss it up and down. If it falls apart it is a very sandy soil. If it stays together you can then squeeze, extrude, roll, and make a muddy mess out of it – and by following a simple checklist you will be able to identify the soil texture. The first few times you do it can be quite messy and you will likely be unsure of yourself, but after you have done a few you will be able to get a very good estimate of the texture very quickly. If you need a more precise estimate there are many soil testing firms that will take your samples and tell you the textures.

Soils can be mapped in terms of their characteristics. The most common categorization is based on texture. As with other resource maps, it is often valuable to have main categories based on something like texture, and then subcategories to identify differences in some other soil characteristic such as compaction. For example, two soils with the same texture will have very different drainage characteristics if one is in a natural situation and one has been compacted by vehicles.

Notes:

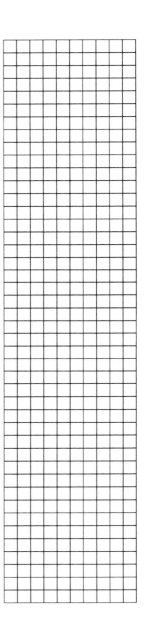

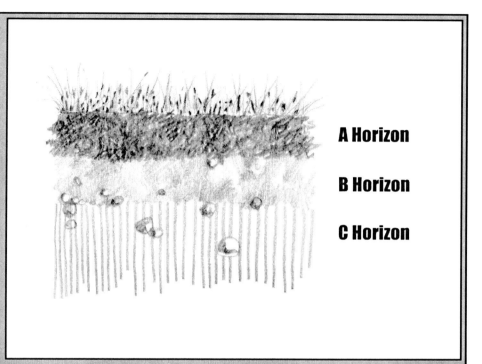

A Horizon

B Horizon

C Horizon

Figure 13 - Soil Horizons

If you dig in undisturbed soil, you will find that it has clearly visible layers. The depths of the layers varies with the soil, but virtually all soils have an A-horizon (commonly known as the topsoil), a B-horizon, and a C-horizon (which is material that has not been modified much by plants and animals).

Notes:

Social and Cultural Elements

Over the past two hundred years or so, settlement of southern Ontario has resulted in the removal or disturbance of almost all naturally-occurring ecosystems. These areas have largely been replaced with cultural landscapes ranging from human settlements to agricultural fields. Small remnants of the original ecosystems still survive, but they are scattered throughout the landscape. Even these are culturally influenced as the outline of remnant forests tend to be determined by surveyed property lines (see Figure 14).

Lands that have been heavily modified by humans tend to have lost much of their former structure and form, but many of the landscape processes are still in place. For example, water still flows downhill, solar radiation remains most intense on south facing slopes, and soils tend to have the topsoil at the surface. Through understanding of the components of ecosystems, you can begin to recreate lost environments. Many of the effects of the landscape processes, however, are magnified by human development. For example, rainwater isn't able to penetrate most concrete and asphalt, so more of it is forced to become runoff. With an increase in the volume of runoff the erosive capacity of the flowing water is also increased, often resulting in erosion of areas downstream of built up landscapes. Similarly, solar radiation reaching a dry concrete or asphalt surface is not able to evaporate water and instead goes into heat production. This can make built areas hotter and drier than a natural area. Plant communities are generally simplified in human dominated areas. For example, the complex web of life in a Maple-Beech forest is often simplified to cultivated trees and grass. The wide array of animal life that depended on the complexity of the original ecosystem can't survive and so disappear along with their habitat.

Notes:

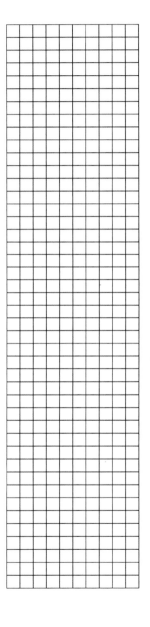

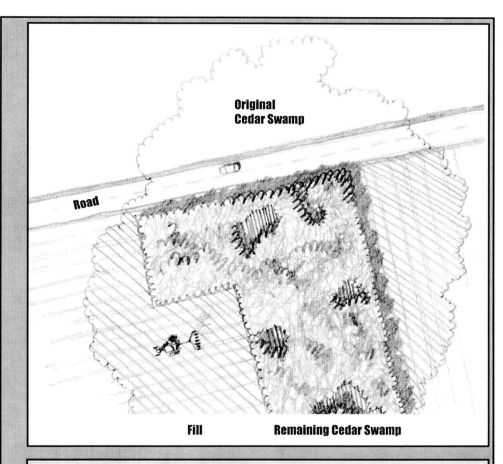

Original
Cedar Swamp

Road

Fill

Remaining Cedar Swamp

Figure 14 - Remnant Landscapes

Remnant 'natural' areas found in the landscape of Southern Ontario are typically regrowth areas. This means that the original vegetation has been removed within the last 200 years or so, and new vegetation has grown there. Where ecosystems in an undisturbed area would naturally follow the environmental conditions (e.g. a cedar wetland will grow to the edges of the wet area), the boundaries of remnant natural areas are more typically determined by surveyed property lines, roads, etc.

Notes:

While some human impacts have been devastating for natural systems, not all signs of human use of the land are negative. Society is often interested in preserving or conserving buildings and landscapes where historic events occurred, such as battle sites from the War of 1812, or where cultural events continue to happen, such as Stratford-Upon-Avon. Other sites of interest are areas of pre-European settlement such as the Longhouse Village at Crawford Lake, Ontario. Any evidence of human intervention in a landscape should be recorded and mapped.

Many characteristics of a landscape are less tangible than the biophysical resources but are still highly valued by society and cultures. People appreciate high points of land that offer views of interesting or beautiful landscapes or communities. They also appreciate opportunities to interact with nature through trails and interpretive signage. People also benefit in many ways, both physically and psychologically, from being in contact with nature. As you are conducting the biophysical inventory of a site, be very aware of intangible human-valued characteristics. These can be mapped in a variety of ways, but can be included as big asterisks or stars on a socio-cultural map. Both the legend and the report can indicate the reason that these points have been identified, and later when you are designing you can take these opportunities into consideration.

When reading a greenfield (undeveloped) landscape look for anything out of the ordinary. Sometimes you will come across plants that would not occur naturally but might indicate a long-abandoned house site. Or you will see mounds of earth that are unlike any natural landform that you know. These can be clues that lead to historic or prehistoric resources on the site such as ancient burial mounds.

When reading a greyfield (has been developed and is going to be redeveloped) landscape you have to look for different things. Look for the patterns in the landscape and the area surrounding the site. Is there a grid pattern? Where are the utility corridors? What lies uphill from the site that might impact the use? What lies downhill that your design might impact?

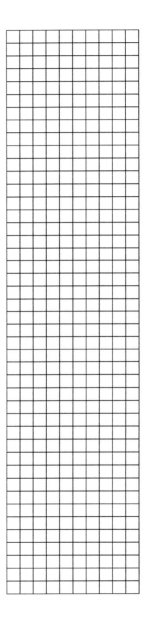

Mapping Landscape Components

Each of the components of the landscape should be mapped and reported in a manner that not only clearly communicates the information about the resource, but does it in a way that a client can readily understand. It should also identify the key information that will direct and influence the design.

The following *process guides* provide step-by-step assistance on what to do when visiting a site, how to develop your base map, and so on. The typical product of a landscape assessment is a report that integrates maps with written description.

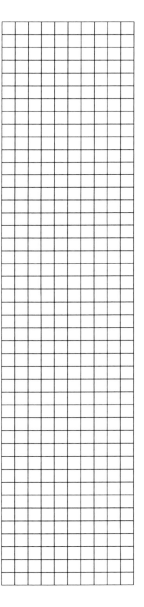

04 Process Guides

Introduction

This chapter provides you with a series of process guides that will assist you in some of the steps in the landscape assessment process. Not all the steps of the landscape assessment process have been included as some aspects are quite straightforward. However, areas where students in past years have had difficulty have been explained in some detail so as to help you along the way. Some time, in the middle of working on a project, you might need to remember what information needs to go onto a base map. You can turn to the section on *Constructing a Base Map* and find the critical information and the steps to make it happen.

The guides have been designed to help you through each process the first time you do it, and to act as a reference in future to remind you of the steps to be taken.

Notes:

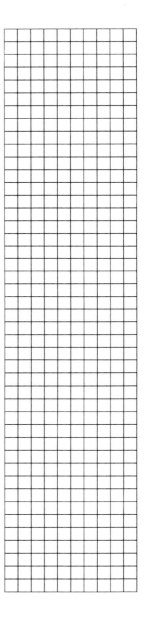

Recording and Reporting Observations

One of the most important processes in landscape analysis is developing skills to accurately report and record observations. Your analysis of a site begins with casual observations and develops into a complex review of information from a number of sources. The process of taking a large amount of information and developing a succinct report can seem quite perplexing. However, by effectively summarizing this information in written and graphical form, the process of developing a final report becomes a simple process - like putting together pieces of a puzzle.

You will report and record observations using a variety of methods such as making notes during site visits, summarizing papers and technical reports, sketching diagrams perspectives and sections, and recording information on maps and air photos. In fact, this important step in project development often takes many forms. You should end up with many notes that will guide you through the process of completing your report. Most importantly, developing this skill will help you to avoid cramming information out at the last minute.

Notes:

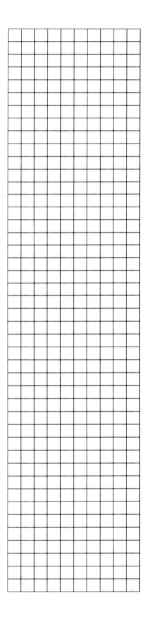

Steps

1.   Buy a hard cover, permanently bound book with lined or graphed paper. Use a pencil, but never erase your ideas and comments. You never know when you will need to jog your memory or spark creative thoughts with a subtle bit of insight. Pencil will not smear or erase if it gets wet.

2.   Take the book with you whenever you work on a given site. Track your work by recording the date each time you work on a site. It is important to chronologically follow your comments and observations. Record any and everything related to the site in this book; ideas, thoughts, suggestions, references etc. Record things the way you understand them best, but remember, others in your office may need to refer to your notes in the future - strive to be clear and thorough.

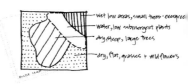

3.   Take photocopies of maps and air photos of the site to each site visit. Track your field investigation accurately with reference to these important tools. Note significant areas of vegetation, important views, steep topography, etc. The process of graphically noting areas of importance and referring to the maps on site will make it much easier to orientate yourself and your ideas off-site.

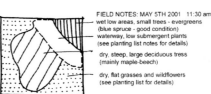

4.   Upon completion of each site visit, review your text and make additional comments. Make sure that all of your notes make sense to you off-site.

FIELD NOTES: MAY 5TH 2001   11:30 am
wet low areas, small trees - evergreens
(blue spruce - good condition)
waterway, low submergent plants
(see planting list notes for details)

dry, steep, large deciduous tress
(mainly maple-beech)

dry, flat grasses and wildflowers
(see planting list for details)

5.   When you review a journal article, paper, technical report or any other material that requires a reference, record all information that will be required for accurately referencing the material at the top of your page of notes. This will typically include the author(s) name, date of publication, title, publisher (or journal name), edition or volume, and page number(s). If you intend to use a quote, ensure that you record the page that it appeared on. After you complete the process of taking notes, take a few minutes to summarize the important points of the paper - things that you feel will be of importance in your report. This may seem tedious, but it will ensure that you have understood what you have recorded and how it will apply to your report.

6. Occasionally synthesize your information to date onto one page (probably based on a map). Mark this page with a tab. Put all relevant information onto that page. You will have several of these pages by the time the project is complete, and find them easily through the tab system.

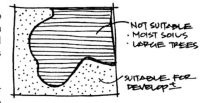

7. Think about your audience - who is going to read your report and maps? Think about what they would need to know, in what order, to be able to really understand the site and know its capabilities and limitations (opportunities and constraints). The more information you accurately gather, the greater opportunity you will have to effectively communicate to your colleagues.

8. Write clearly, and illustrate your text with appropriate diagrams and sketches.

Notes:

Constructing a Base Map

      Throughout your project reports much of your inventory and analysis will be communicated graphically through a series of maps. In order to illustrate a variety of resource information accurately, it is imperative that all of these maps have a consistent format and appearance. That is, all maps must be presented on the same size paper, at the same scale, and show the same base information. A base map is the template for all maps in a given project or report.

Steps

1.   An Ontario Base Map (OBM) can often provide a convenient starting point. It will contain much of the information you will need to develop your base map. You might have to 'cut and paste' maps together if your property is partly on more than one map. Ensure that you accurately locate the boundaries of your property.

1: 10,000

2.   Choose a reasonable scale for your base map. OBMs are at a scale of 1:10,000. If you want or need a different scale for your base map you have to ensure that the enlarging or reducing of the maps is done so as to provide a reasonable scale in the end. For example, you might double the size of your map and end up with a scale of 1:5,000. The scale you decide on for your base map will depend on several things, including the size of paper you intend to use for your maps, the size of the property, and the level of detail you intend to illustrate.

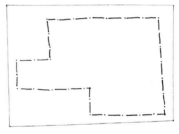

1:5,000

3.   Create a layout for your base map. Items that should **always** be included on a base map are:

-   A graphic scale
-   A north arrow
-   The title of the map
-   Space for a legend
-   The source(s) of the information on the map
-   The date
-   The name of the client
-   The name of the firm doing the study, and
-   The project name and property address.

      Anything else that you want to show up on every map in your set should be included on the base map.

4. Somewhere on your base map you should have a regional context map that illustrates the location of the site in the larger region. It is usually a small, simple sketch (not to scale) showing a few local roadways, and a shadow of the shape of the property. This can be in the legend or part of your title block.

5. The most convenient and accurate means of creating a base map is to use AutoCad. Once you have the whole base map laid out in draft form use a digitizing table to input pertinent information onto your base map layer.

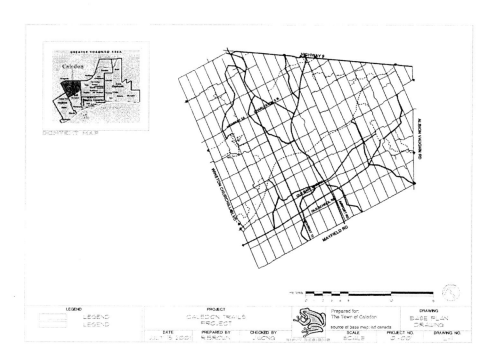

Resolving Scales

All maps simplify the landscape in order to represent it. It is very important to understand the degree to which a map has been simplified by interpreting the scale. Scales are represented on a map in a number of ways, but typically are shown as both a graphic scale and a representative scale.

Resolving Scales

A scale with a small number on the bottom or right-hand side of the equation (*e.g.* 1/100 or 1:100) is known as a fine-scale map. Read this, as 1 unit on the map is equal to 100 units on the ground. You are able to make out quite fine detail on a map of this scale. For example, you would be able to see individual houses in a community.

A scale with a large number on the bottom or right hand side (*e.g.* 1/1,000,000 or 1:1,000,000) is known as a coarse-scale map. Read as 1 unit on the map = 1,000,000 units on the ground. You can make out the overall pattern of a landscape but can't see individual houses on the map as they would be too small to represent.

You might hear others talk about large scale and small-scale maps. This can be confusing because some people refer to a fine-scale map as a 'small scale' as it deals with the details of a small area; others call a fine scale map a 'large scale' as the number (*e.g.* 1/100) is large compared to a 'small scale' map of 1/1,000,000.

Steps

1.   When you gather resource maps for a site, you will almost certainly find maps of different scales. Ensure that you accurately record and source each map you use and the scale at which it is represented.

SOILS MAP   1:10 000

62

2.	Remember that maps at different scales will represent different levels of information. A soils map might be at 1:10,000 while a landforms map might be at 1:250,000. Be aware of the detail of information contained on maps of different scale. In the above example, the soils map will contain more detailed information than would the landforms map. Ideally, you should convert to the scale that shows the least detail. However, this is not always practical, as you often want to show as much information on the site at hand as possible. In order to compensate for the information lost in the conversion and any discrepancies between the information displayed on the two maps, you might have to use a broader line weight to represent the information accurately.

LANDFORM MAP	1:50 000

3.	AutoCAD is a very effective tool for resolving maps of different scales. However, no matter how dependent you become on AutoCAD for converting scales, at times you will need to quickly review information from two maps with different scales at one common scale. For example, you may need to review a map produced at 1:3000 with a map at 1:2000. The easy rule of thumb is to divide the denominator of the original scale, by the denominator on the scale you wish to convert to.

LANDFORM MAP	1:10 000

If you want to convert 1:3000 to 1:2000:

Divide 3,000/2,000 to get 1.5; then multiply by 100 to get a 150%.

Simply enlarge the coarser scale map (1:3000) by 150% on the photocopier

If you wanted to convert a map at 1:2000 to 1:3000:

Divide 2,000/3,000 to get 6.7; then multiply by 100 to get 67%.

Simply reduce the finer scale map (1:2000) by 67% on the photocopier.

Landscape Units

You should now be at the stage where you have performed a detailed site inventory and analysis. You have gathered information on the site's specific resource characteristics, such as landforms, microclimate, soils, water, animals, plants, and history, and represented them on a series of maps. The complexity of information contained within these maps may seem a bit overwhelming. You have taken one site, and systematically divided it into a variety of elements, relating to each specific resource characteristic. Without simplifying this information further, it would be very difficult to make any informed land use decisions. Therefore it is now important that you take this information and communicate it in a simple, concise form. One of the most effective means of conveying a wide variety of resource information is through the use of *landscape units*. Landscape units are displayed on one map and represent a synthesis of specific landscape characteristics. These units provide a simplified basis for developing land use strategies.

Notes:

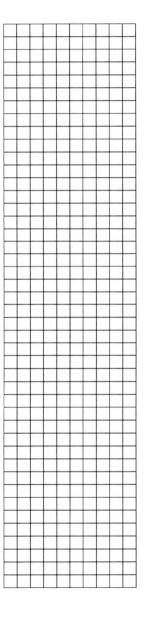

64

Steps

1.   One of the most common means of identifying
landscape units is to overlay, one by one, the information
contained in your resource maps. You need to determine the
relative importance of the resource characteristics to your
overall landscape unit map and the development of your land
use decisions. This process takes experience and ingenuity.
You may have to take some time to develop your
methodology.   There are many means of developing
landscape units, so do not be afraid to experiment and use trial
and error to develop an effective strategy for your individual
project. Remember that the landscape unit map will form the
basis of any land use decisions that you develop for the site.

2.   The following illustrates an example methodology for
developing a landscape unit map.

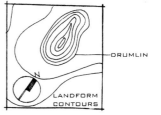

a)   Identify a basis for your decision making process. Bio-
geographical theory suggests that there are identifiable
systems in the landscape. Knowledge of how these systems
work allows us to identify and map the systems or landscape
units on the site.

    For example, a south-facing slope will preserve higher
amounts of solar radiation that will make it warmer and
consequently drier than other slopes. Its microclimate differs
from surrounding slopes. The vegetation on that slope will
consist of plants that prefer or tolerate warmer, drier
conditions and an increased exposure to sunlight. You can
see that the south-facing slope has characteristics that would
be different from every other slope.

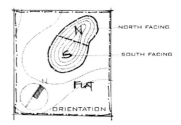

b)   The first step to developing a landscape units map
based on the above theory is to take your **landform** map and
use it as your base. The landforms are essentially the driving
element behind the diversity in the landscape.

    The landforms were acted upon by climate and it is the
slope and orientation of the land that creates the
microclimate. On your landform map identify south-facing,
north-facing, and no slope zones. This can be expanded to
identify east-facing and west-facing, and to include steep
slopes, moderate slopes, and low slopes if appropriate.

c)   The next step is to superimpose the **soil** information onto your map. You should see congruencies between the landforms and soils. If the lines don't quite match up, it is likely due to mapping inaccuracies that resulted from developing the maps from sources at varying scales. Draw the lines a bit wider to accommodate for these inaccuracies.

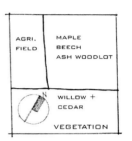

d)   Next superimpose the **vegetation** map. You might want all the detail of the vegetation zones, but this might be the time when you want to collapse categories or otherwise simplify the vegetation. However, retain as much detail as possible and appropriate.

e)   This might give you enough landscape units for your analysis. So far we have identified 6 units. We could add hydrology or other geological physical characteristics to develop finer detail, but through integration of these four maps you might have captured the main elements.

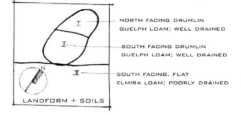

I : FLAT; GUELPH LOAM; WELL DRAINED TILL; AGRICULTURAL FIELD; NORTH FACING

II : FLAT; GUELPH LAOM; WELL DRAINED TILL; MAPLE BEECH ASH WOODLOT

III : DRULIN; GUELPH LOAM; WELL DRAINED TILL; MAPLE BEECH ASH WOODLOT

IV : DRUMLIN; GUELPH LAOM; WELL DRAINED TILL; MAPLE BEECH ASH WOODLOT; SOUTH FACING

V : FLAT; GUELPH LOAM; WELL DRAINED TILL; MAPLE BEECH ASH WOODLOT; SOUTH FACING

VI : FLAT; ELMIRA LOAM; POORLY DRAINED; WILLOW + CEDAR; SOUTH FACING

66

f)   The units should be outlined with a fairly 'fat' line to illustrate the uncertainty of where the boundaries are. Each unit should be coloured in a way to represent the characteristics.   For example, Unit I could be brown to represent fallow fields, Unit II could be medium green to represent forest, the North Slope dark green to represent the rich moist forest and the south slope light green. Do not use colours like pink or fuchsia unless you are representing a field full of flowers!

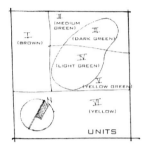

3.   Remember that the idea behind developing a landscape units map is to simplify the categories contained in your resource maps. If you create a landscape units map with 36 units, it should be simplified. There are two approaches to simplifying this map; reduce the number of maps you use in your overlay process, or collapse the number of categories contained within the individual resource maps. It may be most logical to use a combination of these approaches. In general, your landscape units map should contain no more than 10 units.

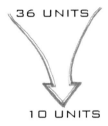

4.   Ensure that you record the process you used to develop your landscape units and explicitly explain your methodology in your report. This should be a step-by-step process providing the reader with a chronological development of your landscape units map. It should explain the theory behind your specific process, each map you used and the order in which they were overlaid, if you collapsed or simplified any of the categories in each map, and your final outcome of categories. You may want to use a flow chart or table to show this process of simplification.

Notes:

Capability and Suitability

Now that you have identified your landscape units, you can now begin to develop your land use recommendations. Remember that you have followed a specific process. It is very important that you stay true to your methodology by basing your land use recommendations on your analysis completed up to this point. Do not abandon your work and make personal assumptions on what is the right or wrong type of development for your site.

A reliable and convenient means of assessing the site's land use potential is by using *capability* and *suitability* analysis. Although these terms may seem very similar, they hold very distinct meanings in terms of land use. Capability is often referred to as the 'raw ability' of the land to support certain land uses. It is an objective means of assessing the landscape. For example, you might argue that forested land shouldn't be developed into housing, but objectively thinking, the forest could be cut down to permit housing development. Therefore, it might be capable of supporting housing. Suitability is a subjective means of assessing the landscape. It addresses the social, economic, environmental and ethical concerns relating to development. Now you can argue that forested land is not suitable for supporting housing because of the ecological value of the forest.

Steps

1.   Use your landscape units map as the starting point. Remember that the units have been developed to simplify and communicate the site's resource characteristics. Think of each landscape unit as being 'horizontally homogeneous'. That is, everywhere within a unit the landscape characteristics are essentially the same. Strictly avoid 'breaking up' the units to represent additional resource components.

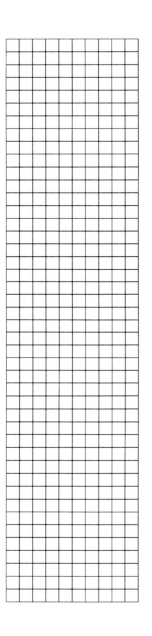

2. A matrix can be a valuable tool for assessing landscape capability and suitability. Matrices can communicate a large amount of information in a convenient, organized and legible manner. To begin, create a table which list all of the units along one axis and all potential land uses on the opposite axis. Ideally, you should consider as many land uses as possible. You can be general (*e.g.* residential) or specific (*e.g.* apartments, single detached homes, townhouses). Be creative and avoid limiting yourself.

Land Uses	Landscape Units					
	Unit I	Unit II	Unit III	Unit IV	Unit V	Unit VI
Agriculture						
Residential						
Commercial						

3. At this point you should define a scale of capability and suitability. Typical descriptors are low, medium and high. This provides a qualitative means of assessing the relative degree of capability and suitability. You should be able to define what low, medium and high degrees of capability and suitability means to give your rating system some credibility. For example, you may base the relative capability on the work that will be required to support certain land uses within that unit.

Notes:

4.   Begin completing your matrix by rating the capability. Take each unit and consider whether it would be capable of supporting each potential land use in turn. Next take each unit and consider whether it would be suitable for supporting each potential land use in turn. You may use a separate table, but it is often easiest to display this information by separating the cells within the matrix.

Land Uses	Landscape Units					
	Unit I	Unit II	Unit III	Unit IV	Unit V	Unit VI
Agriculture	H/L	M/L				
Residential						
Commercial						

The above example is purely hypothetical. Remember that you should provide a brief explanation of the theory behind your decision making process for determining relative degrees of capability and suitability.

5.   After this matrix is complete, analyze it for patterns. Which cells show both high capability and suitability? Medium capability and suitability? Low capability and suitability? A combination of the above? You may begin to separate your land uses into 'categories' based on these ratings. According to the matrix, what are the 'best' and 'worst' uses for each unit.   You may want to create an additional table showing these categories.   Read **across** the matrix to identify the best places for each land use, and read **down** the matrix to identify the best uses for each landscape unit.

6.   The next step is to consider potential land uses for each unit. Assess the results from your matrix, and mark your development options on your Landscape Units Plan. This begins to become the basis for your land use allocation recommendations. You may begin to recognize that there maybe a number of development options in many units. You will begin to explore various land use strategies. It may even be advantageous to develop a number of maps to represent different development options.

Report Writing

Now that you have worked through the process of inventory and analysis, and are ready to present your land use strategies for the site, it is time to prepare your final report. The organization and presentation of this report is the key component to effectively communicating the process that you followed to develop your final land use recommendations. In essence, the quality of your final report determines the credibility of your decisions.

Your final report should provide the reader with a detailed review of the process that you followed to develop your final recommendations and conclusions. Not enough emphasis can be placed on the importance of clearly defining your process. Assume that your readers know nothing about your project. In reality, when you begin your career as a landscape architect, your firm will be working on a number of projects at once. Your colleagues will depend on these reports as the basis for their understanding of the work that is going on within the firm.

Steps

1.   The first thing that should appear in your final report is an Executive Summary (ES). As discussed before, the ES provides a concise summary of the information contained in your final report. Although the ES appears first in your report, it should be the last thing you write. An easy way to write an ES is to summarize each section of your report with one or two succinct sentences. In general, the ES should tell the reader what you did, how you did it, and what your main conclusions/recommendations were. The ES should be no longer than one or two paragraphs, and should not contain personal opinions or judgments.

2.   The Table of Contents should appear next in your report. Ensure that each section is accurately listed with the coinciding page number. In addition to your table of contents, you may wish to provide a list of figures, tables, and/or maps.

71

3.   The introduction to your report should provide the reader with some context as to what you are doing and why you are doing it. To describe why you are doing your project, you may want to provide some historical context as to how your project developed or the issues that render the results of your project unique and of value.   You may provide references to studies that provide some background and substantiate the importance of your project. Keep in mind that the most fundamental component to your introduction is the thesis statement. In one or two sentences, this statement should explicitly state what your project set out to do.

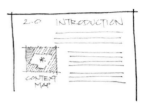

4.   The body of your report should contain sections that explicitly describe the process you followed and a detailed description of your final land use recommendations. Traditionally, the portion of your report describing the process is called the methodology section. Journal articles provide great references for learning how to record your methods concisely and accurately.

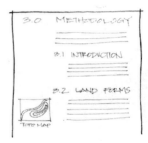

5.   In your methods section, ensure that you describe each step you followed. Start by recording each step in point form (this is where keeping an accurate record of your observations in a log will come in handy). Think about everything you did, and record it, no matter how tedious it may appear. In general you may have:

        Started with theory (*e.g.* landforms, microclimate, vegetative association etc.);

        Referred to published maps and reports (both about the site specifically plus those for the region);

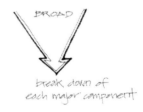

Performed field reconnaissance (i.e. data collection, ground truthing etc.);

Prepared resource mapping;

Assessed landscape capability, suitability; and

Determined land use recommendations.

Take a broad approach to begin with, and then break down every step into detailed descriptions of how you successfully completed each. The key to writing this section is to provide enough information so that the reader could duplicate your process.

6.   The next step is to present your results and discussion as they pertain to the methods that you followed. This is where it becomes imperative that the reader be able to interpret exactly how you came to the conclusions you did.

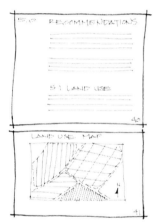

An effective means of presenting this discussion is to break up your text into sections. Use your methods section as a guideline. For example, you may use headings for Inventory and Analysis, Landscape Capability and Suitability, and Land Use Recommendations (with appropriate subheading where needed). This strategy will help you organize your thoughts. Given the amount of information you have gathered, writing a final report can seem overwhelming. In fact, you can take this one step further by breaking up each subheading into a few important points - use these points as guidelines for the structure of your paragraphs.

7.   One of the primary goals of this report was to provide a concrete set of land use recommendations. When you prepare this section, make sure you provide sufficient detail so that the reader is able to understand where every land use recommendation came from and why it was made. You may have prepared a few maps showing different development options. Ensure that you explain why these options exist - provide enough detail to justify your decisions. For clarity, you may wish to explain each option on a separate page. If you can, take this process one step further and define a best development option.

8.   Your maps should provide clarity to the content of your text. The maps should appear next to the sections they are referenced in, rather than at the end of the report. Each map should have a consistent format and orientation. As they were produced from the same base map, they should look like a 'matched set'. If you use colour, it should be appropriate and consistent. If using grey scales on maps, make sure they reproduce clearly and that any patterns relate to the resource characteristic. If you are constrained by time, avoid detailing one map and leaving the rest less detailed and ensure that all maps appear as a consistent set.

9.   Think about the most important points in your report. What impressions, facts and recommendations are you trying to leave the reader with? Not surprisingly, your conclusion should provide the reader with a summary of your report. Like the ES, it should provide reference to each section in your report. But, unlike the ES, it should not be free from opinion. It should provide further support to your findings and place emphasis on any recommendations that were made throughout your report.   Commonly, conclusions contain suggestions for areas of future study and research.   Again, journal articles provide a great reference for reviewing how to write an effective conclusion.

10.   Your report should contain references to any sources that you used for additional information - journal articles, books, maps etc. Source any information that appears in the report which is not your own. That is, any statistic, fact or opinion expressed by another author. In an academic setting, it is extremely important to give credit to others - plagiarism is not viewed upon lightly.

Your report must contain a reference section that lists every source contained in the text of your report in alphabetical order. This is not a bibliography. Do not include materials that you did not directly reference in your report.

11.   The very last section that the final report should contain is an Appendix. Not every report will contain this section, but in some cases it will be of value. You may have done some additional analysis, or have some field notes or photos that should be contained in an appendix. If you include an appendix, you must refer to it within the body of your report.

12.   Put an attractive and informative cover on your report. Include the name of the project, the client's name (spelled correctly!), the name of your firm and the date. The cover will provide a first impression, so make it look attractive. A photograph or drawing that encapsulates the character of the landscape would be appropriate – and lay out the information on the page in a well-composed manner.

Notes:

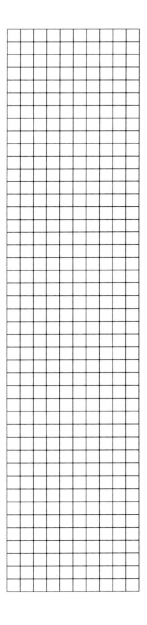

Site Reconnaissance Reports

There are times in consulting offices where a quick, shortened version of an inventory and analysis report is all that is required to get a project started. A site reconnaissance report (SRR) can be used to provide an overview and provide direction for a project.

Landscape architecture firms often send their junior employees out to the site to perform preliminary field studies. The field notes and the report that results from them often become the basis for a more complete site inventory and analysis at a later time. The SRR is quite simply a quick but relatively detailed reconnaissance of the site from which further work can be done. It should include initial site information, photos, maps, notes, and impressions as well as initial notes on the topography, drainage, microclimates and vegetation. Others in the firm should be able to get a very clear sense of the site from the SRR alone, without necessarily having to visit the site. The same landscape architect **might** perform the later site inventory, analysis, and design, but it is equally possible that someone else entirely might be assigned to the project (especially if you, as we hope, have moved up in the firm and are no longer a junior employee!). That means, of course, that your field notes and SRR become the basis from which other people will have to work - so your notes had better be thorough, neat, understandable and accurate.

Notes:

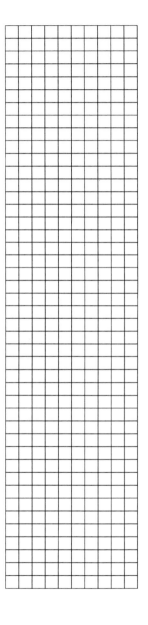

Components

A complete SRR should include a cover page, an executive summary, a table of contents, and a body of the report which consists of both maps and a written report.

Cover Page

The cover page is the first thing that a client (or instructor) is going to see and will provide a first impression. It must include the name of the project and of the client, your name, and the date. It is often advisable to include an image that characterizes the site.

Executive Summary

The executive summary is the first written component in the SRR. It is placed before the Table of Contents and summarizes the findings in the major categories of the SRR. A good way to construct an executive summary is to go through the report and write one or two sentences that summarize each section, and then use those sentences as a basis for your executive summary. Speculation, analysis or design decisions are not appropriate in the executive summary - just include the information you acquired during your site reconnaissance. In case you were wondering, the purpose of the executive summary is exactly as it sounds - a busy executive (or head of the firm) should be able to read just the executive summary to gain an overview of the content of the SRR.

Table of Contents

Each section should be listed with the page numbers on which they begin. This will allow other members of your firm to quickly and easily access that one piece of information they need to refer to about the site.

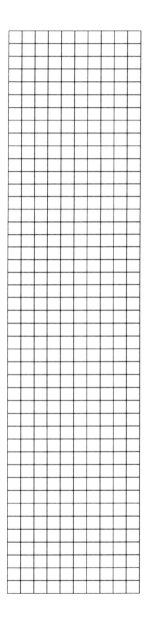

The Body of the SRR

The body of the SRR serves to inform the reader about the site. It should include a broad range of information about the site, but will also include your impressions about the site - even the emotions certain areas of the site evoke. The body of the SRR must also include a description of the process by which you acquired the information and made connections between aspects of the information you gathered.

The body of the SRR should include if possible:

- Notes on the site's history
- Site context and surrounding uses
- Notes on site access
- Observations on the landforms and topography
- Soil observations
- Drainage patterns and problems (try to go see the site on a rainy day so this is clear)
- Microclimates and human comfort observations (going to the site on sunny and windy days would help you here)
- Vegetation notes (Latin names should be used!)
- Observations on wildlife
- Human impact including erosion, pathways, garbage, site damage
- Potential ecologically sensitive areas, especially rare or endangered species and areas that need special attention and study
- Viewsheds, especially notable views that need to be preserved
- Auditory and olfactory observations (what do you hear or smell in areas of the site?)

You should also include photos of the site - include anything you think is important to note – *e.g.* trees, evidence of animal life, pathways and human use, important views etc. In addition, quick (but neat) sketches that convey the information are also helpful.

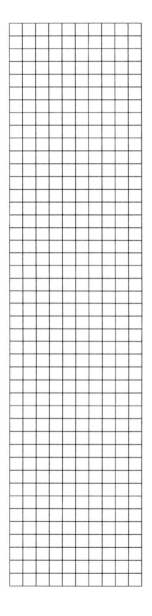

Organizing the Information

First you need to make some decisions about what you think the most effective way of communicating the information to others will be. Do you want to organize the information by topic (see the list above), or by area of the site? If you organize the information by areas of the site, the SRR should have a zone map early on, so that the reader can understand the following sections. How you choose to zone the site will depend upon each site's unique characteristics. For example, you may wish to zone the site according to specific topographical, vegetative, or historical features. If you break the report down by topic, the zone map would logically be placed at the end of the body of the report. Certain firms may have specific guidelines, and in general, other landscape architects may find a SRR organized by site areas easier to follow, but you need to consider the information you have gathered and make your best decision.

Maps

Copies of Ontario Base Maps (OBM), aerial photos, contour maps, soils maps etc. may be included in the SRR. It is completely appropriate to make notes on these maps to highlight important information (just make sure your notes are neat, accurate and readable). All maps should have the same orientation on the page (North should face the same direction), and each should have a North arrow, a scale, the date that it was taken or drawn, and the source. This is important so that others can check or repeat your work. If the source is particularly obscure, put the contact information on the map as well - that way if the firm ever needs to get another example of that particular type of map, they can!

Your own maps are also important. Clearly drawn site maps, with notes, comments, identified views, photos references and sketches that summarize the site's characteristics graphically are particularly informative for other landscape architects. Detail maps for sections of the site may provide much needed insight for later analysis and design decisions. Make sure your maps are clearly labeled and explained. A North arrow is essential, but these particular maps don't need to be drawn to scale.

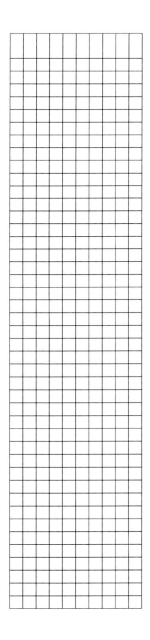

Your SRR must include a clearly labeled zone map that identifies distinct areas of the site based on your site reconnaissance. This site map will serve as the basis for the detailed site inventory that will be performed next. The zone map should be well labeled, clearly drawn and include support for the decisions you have made in terms of identifying the zones on the site. This map might also refer the reader to sections of the report for supporting information. The zone map should be drawn to scale, with the scale clearly indicated. Remember that your report could be read by many different people, so the scale should be common (*e.g.* 1:100; 1:200; 1:500; 1:1000) and clearly labeled graphically and numerically.

Appendices

Articles: If you have found copies of newspaper articles or academic articles about the site, copy them and include them in the SRR. Make sure you indicate the source and date of the articles.

Field Notes: All your field notes should be appended at the end of the SRR. This is important since your on-site observations may contain some crucial insights that determine the outcome of the project. Equally important however, is the fact that the other people who work on the project need to see what you have done, when you did it, and how you started your analysis of the site. This means, of course, that your field notes should be neat, clear, understandable and thorough. You should also record the date, time, and general weather conditions on each site visit as it could directly reflect upon your field observations. When you make notes, take them in a format that can be later bound into your SRR, and make sure they are clear and well labeled.

Notes:

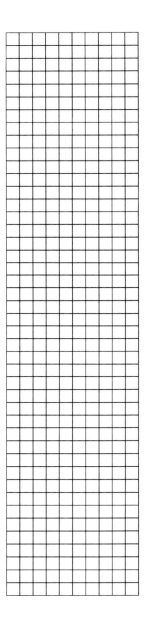

Steps in the Process

The following section outlines a process that can be followed in preparing an SRR. It is important that your process is repeatable and transparent – someone else should be able to follow your written description of your process and come up with essentially the same result.

1.	First time experiencing a site - visit the site; walk through and around it; listen; smell; 'experience' the site - see what the site 'says' to you. This is a very experiential exercise.

2.	Look at a map to see where the site is located within the larger landscape. Regional site context is extremely important to future design decisions. Remember land uses change quickly in urban fringe areas - make sure your map is recent; otherwise you are looking at the history of the site not the site context! Note roads, access and adjacent land uses. Mark a distance roughly 5 times the size of the site in each direction and use this larger area to give an idea of the site's context. Take a photocopy of various maps, and sketch directly on them to graphically note the surrounding land uses. Sketching directly onto the maps will simplify the process of summarizing your visit when you are back in the office.

Site Context Map

See what is within that context area - housing; roads; industry, agricultural fields; forested areas etc. Do some simple area calculations of different land uses in this context area (%). Note the even larger context - adjacent urban areas, typical agricultural uses, tourist attractions of interest, significant natural features in the larger area, etc.

81

3.   Look at the site on aerial photographs (in stereo if available). Imagine that you are flying over the site in a hot air balloon and gaze down at the site for some time. Even better - book a hot air flight and experience this first hand! Do you see any patterns? Lay a sheet of acetate over the air photo and mark off any pattern that you see. Be aware that some areas have excellent air photos that are retaken every few years. Ontario is not one of those areas, however, and some air photos are very out of date. They are still useful for a historical overview of the site uses, but less useful for current site examinations. However, you could try to contact local municipal planning departments to get additional information on sites, and even some recent aerial photograph.

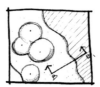

Sketch Plan of moisture - with cross section

4.   Visit the site and take along copies of your map, air photos, plus a field notebook (hard-cover, bound) and a pencil.

See if you can find your 'patterns' on the ground (eg. find the edge of a forest; find your present location on the air photo; find a specific large tree; see if you can identify the tree; find a place where the forest changes from large canopied trees to smaller canopies trees; try to figure out, on the ground, what is happening there; 'ground truth' your air photo interpretation by seeing if your lines/patterns exist on the ground; note if there is any other evidence of change besides vegetation (eg. do soils change, landforms? moisture? etc.)

Sketch Plan - Noise from cars

In your field notebook use a sketch plan to orient your notes. Sketch and make notes directly on the copies of your maps and air photos. In places where the patterns change, or the landscape character changes, you might want to draw a 3-D sketch or cross section to record what is observed. This is especially important on sites that have varying topographical or vegetative features.

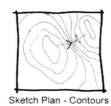

Sketch Plan - Contours

5.   Review your field notes and redraw key maps. If you have made notes directly onto copies of your maps and air photos in the field, this is the step that you will find transferring the information onto your own map much more efficient than if you were to start with a blank slate. You are trying to identify the patterns you observe on the site and trying to understand and explain why those patterns might be there.

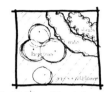
Sketch Plan - Vegetation zones

        The result should be a synthesis map that integrates all your observations and starts to give an overall picture of the site. It should indicate something about each of the following resources for each area: topography, soils, moisture, vegetation (type, age, size etc.), slope, and anything else that defines the area.

ZONE 1. wet, low areas,
small canopied tress: evergreens
ZONE 2. water: low,submergent plants
ZONE 3. dry, steep, large trees
– deciduous maple and beech
ZONE 4. Dry, flat, grasses and wild flowers

Synthesis Map

6.   Now that you have the patterns identified - visit the site again. This time start by checking that your zones or patterns make sense.   Then, within each zone, look for differences - things that don't fit the pattern. This is when you might find a rare plant, or an animal den or an unusual landform - note these unusual features within the pattern.

7.   The site may contain locations that offer views of unique features or great landscapes. If there are spectacular views you might note them with a symbol.

Special Features Map

8.   You may begin to think about how this site might be used. The site may lend itself to obvious uses - for human development?   For natural regeneration?   For education? Interpretation? Think about what the site is composed of and how these characteristics will help or hinder various uses?

Notes:

05 Connection to Design

After having undertaken data collection, analysis, synthesis, and general assessment of the landscape, you are ready to apply the information to planning and design of the land. There are many different ways of approaching this, and you will find that for you some techniques will work better than others. Try any or all of them for any given design problem. The more you explore the relationship between landscape and design, the more complete and appropriate will be your design.

Most of the following approaches are *from the ground up* in nature. That is, they use the information that has been determined about the landscape to guide the proposed uses of the land. The final method in the series, functional diagrams, takes more of a 'program down' approach. This approach is useful when there is a definite program that has to be achieved on the site.

Doing What the Land Tells You

Start with the landscape units maps that you developed. Take the information from the capability and suitability analysis and identify what you consider to be, and can justify as, the most appropriate use for each unit. This would be the use that would be most compatible with the biological and physical structures of the unit, and would fit into the evolutionary and successional processes on the land. For example, a mature Maple-Beech forest might be used for maple syrup production, plus it might be appropriate for selective removal of mature trees with high market value such as Black Cherry (*Prunus serotina*) and Black Walnut (*Juglans nigra*). Cropped land near a residential area or near a road might be appropriate for use as a settlement area. If you decided to recommend building houses here, you could provide guidelines into what form the housing might take (*e.g.* clusters of houses on the least productive lands), what amount and kinds of roads (*e.g.* a narrow shared road into each housing cluster, paved with porous asphalt, with the road to be gravelled in winter but no salt to be used, sides of roads planted to vetch and left to grow without chemicals), and the use of the open-space lands (*e.g.* community gardens, natural regeneration areas), and so on.

The program elements as identified by the client should guide you in making your decisions, but the recommendations for the use of the land will come primarily from the land itself. You will likely know the land better than anyone else by the time you have completed your assessment, and will be in a position to make recommendations for the land that would be appropriate for the land and that the owner might never have thought of.

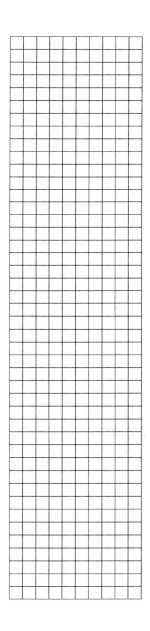

Principles in Practice

In this technique the whole landscape and then each of the landscape units is taken, in turn, and considered in terms of principles. A principle can be either (1) a rule concerning the functioning of natural phenomena, or (2) an essential quality determining intrinsic nature. You will use both kinds of principles in making design decisions.

The first kind of principle would relate to the six natural landscape elements that you studied in the initial assessment (*i.e.* landforms, climate, water, vegetation, animals, and soils). You should attempt to make everything in your design 'fit into' the natural structures and processes of the landscape. To ensure that this happens, state the principles by which the landscape is functioning, so that any design ideas can be tested against these principles to see if they are appropriate. An example of this would be:

The wetland and stream are part of an important hydrologic system that should be preserved.

The wetland retains stormwater and allows it to slowly seep into the groundwater. The groundwater comes to the surface again as a series of springs that slowly and consistently feed the stream. If this wetland were disturbed, stormwater would enter the stream directly and quickly. This could cause damaging erosion of the stream channel, siltation downstream, and might leave the stream dry much of the year.

You can see how this principle would guide any development of the wetland and/or the stream. If someone decided to modify the wetland, they would understand the consequences that they would have to mitigate.

The second kind of principle, "an essential quality determining intrinsic nature", has more to do with the character that you would like the landscape to have when you can complete your design. What attributes, elements, and characteristic behaviour do you want the landscape to have? An example of this kind of principle would be:

Orient living spaces to the south and provide an overhang.

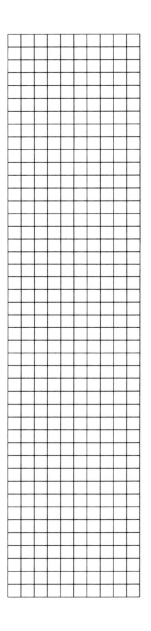

Places where people will be outdoors should be open to the south to allow for solar access. Houses should have their main living spaces and most of their windows on the south sides, and solar access should not be obstructed by other structures. To make the solar access as functional as possible in all seasons, an overhead structure should be provided to block the sun in the summer when it is high in the sky, but allow sun to enter the space in other seasons when it is lower in the sky.

Once you have lists of principles developed that will ensure appropriate development of the landscape, use these to guide your design.

Notes:

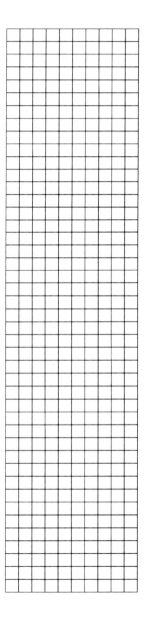

Increasingly Fine-Scale Assessment

In this approach you take each landscape unit, in turn, and conduct a more detailed landscape assessment leading to a finer-scale landscape units map. You will know when you have gone far enough when your units are about the size of your program elements. For example, you might have identified a landscape unit as both capable and suitable for housing, a use that your client is enthusiastic about. Start to investigate this unit in more detail. If you map the slopes and aspects at a finer scale you might begin to see some areas emerge as south-facing slopes, an ideal location for a house site. Flat areas are generally easier to build roads on, and the pattern of the flat areas on your site might provide you with an opportunity to design an interesting drive into the site.

Existing vegetation might provide clues as to where a park might go. When you investigate in detail the vegetation in a patch you might find that it is primarily Norway Maple (*Acer platanoides*) an invasive species that shades out native plants. In this case it would have little ecological value, and could readily be turned into an urban park that would withstand considerable foot traffic and disturbance. Another vegetation patch might turn out to be a very diverse natural area with uncommon or rare plant species. This information would assist you in recommending that the area be conserved, and people might be discouraged from using it at all.

Other patterns that might emerge as you continue to look in more and more detail at the site are areas that are appropriate for septic fields, corridors for overhead lines where the visual blight would not spoil important views, areas of particularly good soil where community gardens might be located, and so on. Let the natural character of the land provide form for your design. There will be lots of room for creativity as most land would be appropriate for many different activities and uses. It will be like solving a puzzle where there are an infinite number of solutions, some of which are more appropriate than others.

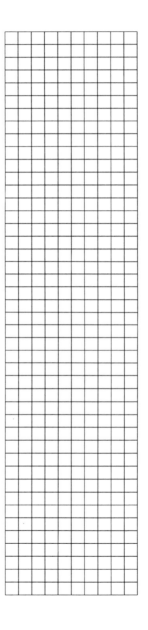

Designing the Ideal Ecological Landscape

If you are studying a landscape that either has tremendous ecological integrity and value, or you have a client who wants to return land to a naturalized state, turn the tables and consider the ecosystem to be your 'client'. What would be the very best thing to do in terms of the landforms, microclimate, water, vegetation, animals, and soils of the site? Take each landscape unit, in turn, and determine what the natural ecosystem was before it was disturbed. Then look at the whole landscape and see how the different ecosystems interact with each other. Use principles of *landscape ecology* to plan and design how the ecosystems interact, and use restoration techniques to recommend how the land can be returned to a more 'natural' state.

Notes:

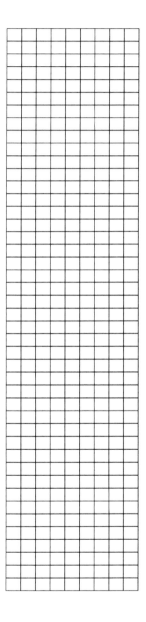

Goals and Objectives

Based on your assessment of the landscape, write out some clear goals that you hope your design will achieve. Make them specific enough that you will be able to tell later whether they were achieved or not, but general enough that they don't become objectives. Objectives are more specific than goals, and relate directly to goals. They tend to be more readily achieved and can be easily tested.

An example might be a landscape where there is a large amount of high quality aggregate, but much of it is below the water table. Extracting the gravel would essentially create a lake. One of our goals might be:

The gravel extraction process should not impact on the water quality of the nearby stream.

Another goal might be:

The lake that is created by the gravel extraction process should be designed to have maximum ecological integrity.

Let's look at the objectives that might go along with each of these goals.

Goal 1: The gravel extraction process should not impact on the water quality of the nearby stream.

Objectives:
- Gravel extraction should not take place within 100m of the stream
- Settling ponds must be used to remove silt from water. The amount of silt in the water exiting the settling ponds must be equal to that in the stream
- Natural vegetation within 50m of the stream must not be disturbed

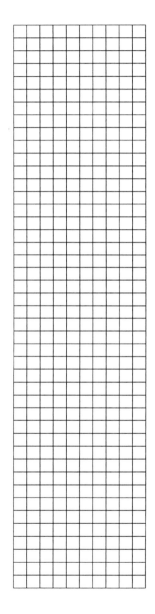

90

Goal 2: The lake that is created by the gravel extraction process should be designed to have maximum ecological integrity.

Objectives:
- The slope of the lakebed, from the shore to 10m into the lake, should be no steeper than 1:10
- A 10m band around the lake should be planted to native plant materials that will be expected to mature within 5 years
- An outlet from the lake should pass through a wetland area before entering the stream

The goals and objectives are developed from the landscape assessment, and guide development of the land.

Notes:

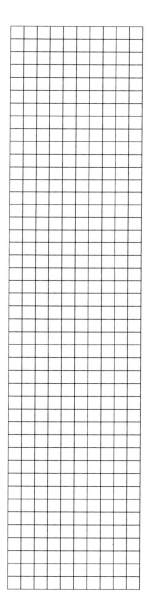

Performance Criteria

In this approach you state how the final outcome should perform, through a series of criteria, and leave the details of how this is achieved to the creativity of the designer. These criteria can be categorized and should be clearly related to the landscape assessment.

An example might be an area that has a functioning, natural wetland, as well as some Class 1 agricultural land.

Ecological Performance Criteria:

- A wetland no smaller than exists at present should continue to function in a natural state (note that this would allow the designer to destroy the existing wetland and create a new one elsewhere on the property)
- Non-native plant species should not be introduced into the wetland as a result of development
- The wetland should be connected via a functioning corridor to the system of wetlands adjacent to the property

Agricultural Performance Criteria:

- Class 1 agricultural lands must not be made unavailable for agriculture (note that this does not require that the land be used for agriculture, only that it not be put in such a state that it could not be returned to agriculture at some future time)
- Chemical fertilizers, herbicides and pesticides should not enter the wetland via agricultural activities

This approach provides the designer with more flexibility. For example, if the wetland is in the most valuable portion of the site, say adjacent to a main road, it can be destroyed to allow the development of a commercial plaza. However, somewhere else on the property the owner must create a wetland at least as large and ecologically important as the existing one. It would be expensive, but it might be economically worth it.

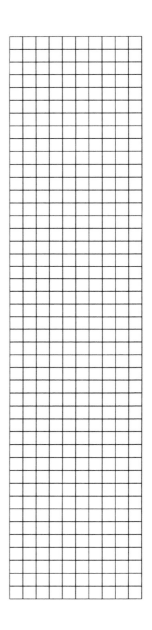

Design Guidelines

Design guidelines are similar to some of the other approaches such as principles or goals and objectives. However, there is one important difference: the statements made in this approach are directly related to how the design and construction should be done. The advantage to using design guidelines is that it more clearly directs the design, and can be traced directly back to the landscape assessment so as to justify and explain design decisions.

Design guidelines can be developed for everything from ecologically-important actions to health-related issues to quality of life amenities.

Ecological Design Guidelines:

- Natural areas should be preserved with no development allowed
- The size of natural areas should be maximized, and the shape should be as nearly circular as possible
- The edges of natural areas should not be undulating, but rather should be as straight a line as possible, following natural systems where appropriate. The edge should have a buffer zone of at least 10m that is planted with low-growing, prickly shrubs and vines to discourage entry by humans.
- Existing trees larger than 0.2m d.b.h. (diameter at breast height) must be protected within their drip line during all construction.
- Construction should not occur within 10m of natural areas.

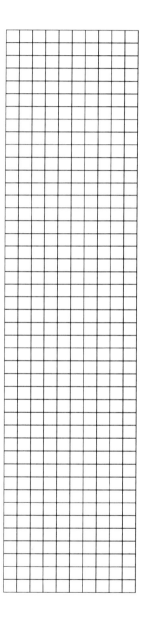

Health-Related Guidelines:

- Lyme disease is not uncommon in this area. Trails through natural areas should have signage that clearly identifies the risks. Trails should consist of aggregate and should be at least 2m in width.
- Vegetation should be pruned regularly so that people walking on the trails will not inadvertently come in contact with any leaves or branches.
- All public buildings, particularly hospitals and retirement facilities, should have gardens that can be viewed from every room. Views of natural landscapes have been shown to help people recover from surgery more quickly, as well as lower heart rate and blood pressure.

Quality of Life Guidelines:

- Views of the natural areas and of the river should be maintained, particularly from public buildings.
- Outdoor use areas should be designed to modify the microclimate so that they will be comfortable in all seasons.
- Areas should be oriented to the south, and should have an overhead structure or overhang of at least 2m so as to block the summer sun but allow the winter sun to penetrate.
- Windbreaks of coniferous vegetation - preferably Eastern White Cedar (*Thuja occidentalis*) trees planted .5m on centre - should be located to the west and north of outdoor use areas.
- The modified wetland should be maintained as a location for people to interact with nature.
- An interpretation facility with boardwalks would provide access for school groups as well as for the general public.

The guidelines that you develop should be kept close at hand during design. If anyone questions why certain decisions were made, you can trace the guidelines back to your assessment and provide them with the rationale.

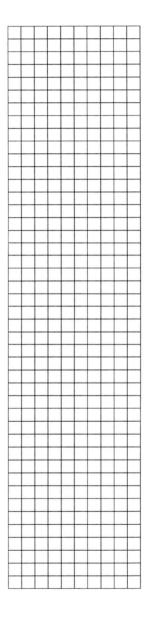

94

Functional Diagrams

Start with the program elements that have been identified by the client. These might include elements like residential units, a golf course, a waste-disposal site, industrial land, parkland, a swimming pool, a formal garden, etc. Write each element from the client's list on a big piece of paper and draw a circle around each element. When all the elements are on the paper, begin to look for relationships between elements by drawing lines between circles. When you find a relationship, either positive or negative, identify it in some way.

For positive relationships (things that might be compatible next to each other) draw a line connecting them, and for negative relationships draw some kind of barrier between the two circles. The residential units and the waste-disposal site would likely be considered incompatible (people don't like to live near a dump) and so a squiggly line might be drawn between the two to show that they should be kept separate. The residential units and the golf course, however, might be quite compatible. In fact, putting them adjacent to each other can enhance the value of both the housing and the golf course. In this case you might want to redraw your circles, moving the two circles closer together, maybe even making them fit together. Continue with this exercise, looking for relationships that work well together as well as those that might potentially lead to something interesting or exciting. Someone had to have been the first person to think that golf and housing might work together. Maybe you can see a way that residential units and industrial lands could work together. For example, it could be light industrial, the complex could include homes designed in harmony with the industry, and it could save the residents from having to commute to work every day. Use the bubble to explore all kinds of ideas, and let your imagination and creativity run wild.

Once you have redrawn your bubbles many many times, and are getting to the point where you are quite happy with the relationships, turn to your landscape units map. Make each landscape unit a bubble and write in it all the opportunities and constraints that your assessment has identified. Identify the best uses, plus those that could be accommodated given the right safeguards.

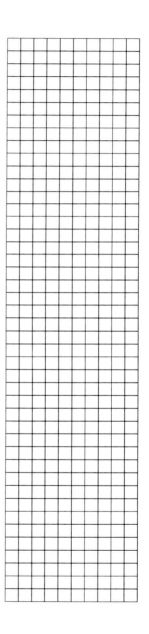

Now take your relationships from the program, and try to fit it onto the landscape units map. It will probably not seem to fit at first, but as you work away at it look for creative ways to accommodate the activities and facilities of the program on your site in such a way that the relationships will still hold, and the integrity of the landscape is conserved.

People sometimes give up prematurely, saying that 'they just don't fit'. However, if you persist and force your mind to find ways to make them to fit, they eventually will. And it might be in a way that you would never have guessed or even considered when you began the exercise.

Notes:

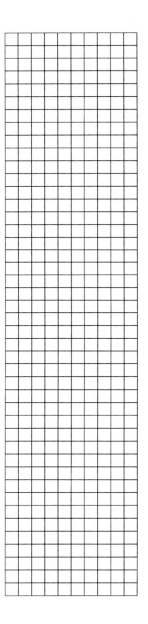

06 Summary

Landscape assessment is the foundation of landscape architecture. It is the process by which landscape architects become familiar with a landscape and by which they communicate the knowledge that they have gained. It also forms the foundation for design recommendations. It is important to remember that landscape architects *do not typically make land use decisions* – they *provide recommendations* to people who either own the land or are elected to make land use decisions. So the recommendations must make sense to the decision-makers or they will likely not be implemented.

Make your case as compelling as possible. Describe the landscape in a way that decision-makers can fully understand the important components of the landscape and are clear that you have made very appropriate land use recommendations. Augment your case with all the skills and knowledge available to landscape architects – use graphic communication skills to make the maps and drawings appealing yet informative, use well-written reports to describe the various components of the landscape and explain why certain land use decisions are more appropriate than others, and provide design recommendations that are creative, imaginative, and of benefit to the decision-makers, the landscape, and the public good.

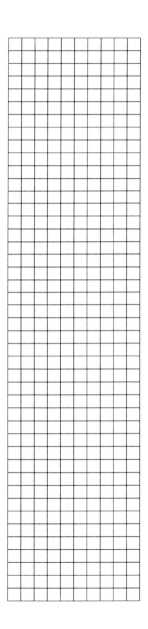

CPSIA information can be obtained at www.ICGtesting.com
Printed in the USA
BVOW03s0447060715

407303BV00007B/99/P